MARITIME
FLAVOURS

Formac Publishing Company Limited acknowledges the support of the Cultural Affairs Section, Nova Scotia Department of Tourism and Culture. We acknowledge the financial support of the Government of Canada through the Book Publishing Industry Development Program (BPIDP) for our publishing activities.

PHOTO CREDITS:

Photographs by Keith Vaughan except where noted below: Janet Kimber, page 14; Len Wagg, page 72; Meghan Collins, page 85; Julian Beveridge, pages 134 (top).

Map by Peggy McCalla.

Library and Archives Canada Cataloguing in Publication

Elliot, Elaine, 1939-
       Maritime flavours guidebook & cookbook : with recipes from the Maritime provinces' finest inns and restaurants / Elaine Elliot and Virginia Lee. — 7th ed.

Includes index.

ISBN 978-0-88780-768-8

       1. Cookery—Maritime Provinces. 2. Restaurants—Maritime Provinces—Guidebooks. 3. Hotels—Maritime Provinces—Guidebooks. I. Lee, Virginia, 1947- II. Title.

TX715.6.E524 2008   641.59715   C2007-907502-9

Formac Publishing Company Limited
5502 Atlantic Street
Halifax Nova Scotia B3H 1G4
www.formac.ca

Distributed in the U.S. by
Casemate
2114 Darby Road, 2nd Floor
Havertown, PA 19083

Printed in China

*This book is dedicated to our children:
Gordon, Stephen and Robert Elliot
and Kate, David and Elizabeth Lee.*

MARITIME FLAVOURS

Guidebook & Cookbook

ELAINE ELLIOT AND VIRGINIA LEE

PHOTOGRAPHY BY KEITH VAUGHAN

Formac Publishing Company Limited
Halifax

CONTENTS

PREFACE

Fourteen years have elapsed since the first edition of *Maritime Flavours* was published. During that time it has become a treasured cookbook and a trusted travel guide. This seventh edition includes dozens of new recommendations to inns and restaurants in the Maritime provinces. As in previous editions, this book is filled with beautiful scenic photos of our three Maritime provinces – New Brunswick, Nova Scotia and Prince Edward Island.

We have made every effort to update the guidebook section of this edition so that it reflects changes as they occur in the hospitality industry. It is our desire to include something for all tastes – from restaurants offering vegetarian and lighter fare to family dining and vacation options, as well as upscale eateries, intimate inns, fishing lodges and elegant resorts. Some establishments were chosen because of their close proximity to historical areas, others because they offer an opportunity to enjoy the rural Maritime experience, far from the bustling tourist crowds. The information included in this book is current at the time of publication, but to ensure our choices meet your personal needs and expectations, we encourage speaking with your hosts before booking reservations. You will note the inclusion of web sites, thus allowing easy access to many of our selections. *Maritime Flavours* is an independent cookbook and guide. No fees have been paid and no benefits received for inclusion.

To maintain the integrity of the book we have left the recipe section intact. Original chefs and establishments remain credited with their creations, though many chefs have moved on, and some establishments have closed. We feel the recipes chosen mirror the unique cuisine of the region with their emphasis on seafood from our waters and produce from our gardens. Each recipe has been carefully selected and tested for home use, and many are accompanied by attractive, full-colour photographs. We invite you to prepare these dishes in your home, and offer this book as a celebration of the beauty of the Maritime provinces and the quality of its cuisine.

— *E.E. and V.L.*

Surfside Inn, Queensland.

1 APPETIZERS

Classic French cookbooks rarely devote much space to appetizers because it is felt a good cook has the experience and imagination to create his or her own. We feel this may be just a little presumptuous; not everyone has sufficient knowledge of sauces, pastries and the like to be confident to mix, match and create a ravishing gastronomic first course.

We have selected a variety of appetizers from the fine chefs of our Maritime restaurants. Some are extremely simple to prepare while others require a little more time and care. All are delicious and well worth the effort.

Appetizers should appeal to your senses. When guests walk through your door they should be welcomed with a wonderful aroma, something that entices the taste buds. The hearty garlic tomato of *Eggplant Parmigiana* and *Bruschetta* from Café Chianti or the delicate herbal aroma of *Mussels Provençale on Toast* from the Walker Inn will heighten their expectations. Other appetizers such as *Seafood Cocktail* from the Rossmount Inn and *Chicken Satay with Peanut Sauce* from Tattingstone Inn have wonderful eye-appeal.

We have included appetizers that are quick and easy, like *Vegetable Crudités* from the Manor Inn, and *Lobster Stuffed Mushroom Caps* from McCrady's Acres, as well as more challenging fare like *Danish Blue Cheesecake in a Walnut Crust with Port Wine Pear Coulis and Spicy Pear Mint Chutney* from the Inn at Bay Fortune.

By increasing the portions of some appetizers, such as *Charbroiled Digby Scallops with Citrus Vinaigrette* from Keltic Lodge, you can easily have a light main course or luncheon dish. Conversely, certain recipes in this cookbook, particularly in the meat, seafood and vegetable sections, when served in smaller portions, make excellent appetizers.

We hope that you will enjoy trying these recipes and perhaps gain a little of that "French confidence" to experiment.

Chicken Satay with Peanut Sauce (Tattingstone Inn)

CHICKEN SATAY WITH PEANUT SAUCE
Tattingstone Inn

At Tattingstone Inn, this wonderful satay with its subtle peanut flavour is served as an appetizer. However, it would make an excellent luncheon dish accompanied by tossed salad and fresh rolls.

1 small red pepper
1 small green pepper
1 small onion
1 pound boneless chicken breast, cut in
    3/4-inch cubes
4 mushrooms
orange and lemon slices
1 tablespoon butter
1 tablespoon flour
salt to taste
pinch of cayenne
1/2 cup warm milk
1/2 cup peanut butter
3 tablespoons white wine
shredded lettuce

Cut peppers into 3/4 inch square chunks, and onion in quarters. Thread chicken pieces and vegetables on four wooden skewers, until all the chicken is used up. Bake the satays at 375°F, 15 to 20 minutes or until chicken is no longer pink in the center.

While chicken is cooking, prepare white sauce. Melt butter in saucepan over low heat, and blend in flour, salt and cayenne. Add warm milk all at once. Heat quickly, stirring constantly, until mixture thickens and bubbles. Remove from heat.

Combine peanut butter and white wine with white sauce, and keep warm. If sauce appears too thick, add a little more milk.

To serve, shred lettuce on four appetizer plates. Place satay on lettuce, garnish with thin lemon and orange slices; drizzle with peanut sauce. Serves 4.

EGGPLANT PARMIGIANA
Café Chianti

One would like to duplicate the aromas that waft from the kitchen at Cafe Chianti. By preparing their version of Eggplant Parmigiana it is possible to create those wonderful hearty garlic, tomato and herb fragrances at home.

1 large garlic clove, crushed
1 1/2 teaspoon fresh basil (1 teaspoon dried)
1 1/2 teaspoon fresh oregano (1 teaspoon dried)
dash of salt and pepper
1 medium eggplant, cut in 1/2-inch slices
1 1/2 cups **tomato sauce** (see below)
1 1/2 cups Parmesan cheese (freshly grated)
black olives, red pepper and green onion, for garnish
olive oil

Combine garlic and seasonings and rub into eggplant slices. Arrange eggplant in bottom of 9 x 12-inch shallow casserole dish, overlapping edges if necessary. Spoon tomato sauce over eggplant and sprinkle Parmesan cheese. Bake at 425°F for 10 to 15 minutes until the eggplant is soft and the sauce bubbly.

Serve on individual dishes. Garnish with black olives, sliced red pepper and julienne green onions which have been tossed in olive oil. Serves 6.

Tomato Sauce
This versatile tomato sauce is a wonderful alternative to the store–bought canned version. It can be used in any recipe calling for a basic tomato sauce. If prepared in larger quantities, it can be frozen for future use.

1/4 cup olive oil
3/4 cup Spanish onion, finely chopped
1 can Italian plum tomatoes (28 ounces)
1/4 teaspoon salt
4-5 turns of pepper grinder

Sauté onion in oil until transparent. Add tomatoes and seasoning and simmer on low heat for 1 hour. Near the end of the cooking time, whisk to break up the tomato. If sauce is too liquid, thicken with a paste of flour and cold water; if too thick, add water. Makes 2 1/2 cups.

VEGETABLE CRUDITÉS
The Manor Inn

An assortment of crisp, fresh vegetables makes this an easy eye-appealing appetizer. In testing we substituted light sour cream and mayonnaise with excellent results.

1 cup sour cream
2 tablespoons mayonnaise
1 tablespoon fresh dill, chopped
1 teaspoon parsley, chopped
1/8 teaspoon lemon juice

Fresh crisp vegetables in bite–size pieces (e.g. carrots, celery, zucchini, broccoli, cauliflower, mushrooms).

Combine dip ingredients and place in a dish in the center of a platter. Arrange an assortment of vegetables in an attractive fashion around dip. Serves 4 to 6.

BRUSCHETTA
Café Chianti

In the Tuscany area of Italy, dinner begins with a classic "Bruschetta"; a slice of toasted bread spread with garlic and covered with olive oil, tomato slices and basil leaves. Café Chianti's version makes a delicious appetizer or accompaniment to a main course.

1 1/4 cups Spanish onion, finely chopped
2 large, ripe tomatoes, chopped
1/2 cup olive oil
1 tablespoon fresh basil, chopped (1 teaspoon dried)
1 teaspoon fresh oregano, chopped (1/2 teaspoon dried)
1 garlic clove, minced
1 loaf of Italian bread, cut in half, lengthwise
Italian cheese, grated or crumbled

Combine onion, tomatoes, oil, basil, oregano and garlic and mix well. Spread mixture evenly over sliced sides of bread. Top with an Italian cheese such as Boccinni, unripened mozzarella, Romano, Asaigo or Parmesan.

Bake uncovered on a cookie sheet in preheated 425°F oven for 5 to 6 minutes or until browned and bubbly. Slice to serve.

STEAK TARTARE
The Rossmount Inn

Chefs at the Rossmount Inn find that a fine beef tenderloin, minced and seasoned in the traditional manner, satisfies the most discerning palate.

8 ounces beef tenderloin, cubed
1 tablespoon onion
5 drops Tabasco sauce
7 drops Worcestershire sauce
1/2 egg yolk
5 capers
1 anchovy fillet
salt and pepper
1 teaspoon brandy
chopped fresh parsley
rye bread

Chop the beef very finely, or carefully pulse in a food processor until it is finely ground; remove to a bowl. Process onion, sauces, yolk, capers and anchovy until finely chopped and add to meat. Combine the ingredients in the bowl until they are well blended. Season with salt and pepper to taste. Shape the tartare into a patty and place on a serving dish. Pour brandy over top, garnish with parsley and serve with thin slices rye bread. Serves 4.

SEAFOOD COCKTAIL
The Rossmount Inn

Rossmount Inn steps away from the traditional seafood cocktail served with a tomato–based sauce and instead, offers guests an interesting variation with scallops, shrimp and mussels served in a Dijon-styled vinaigrette. The results is elegant, delicious and easy to prepare.

1 cup water
1/4 cup dry white wine
1 bay leaf
5 black peppercorns
1/4 small onion
1 celery stalk, quartered
24 mussels
12 scallops, halve if large
12 shrimp, peeled and deveined
vinaigrette
6 tomato slices
6 cucumber slices
shredded lettuce
6 lemon wedges
fresh parsley, chopped

In a large pot combine first 6 ingredients, and bring to a boil. Poach mussels for 2 minutes and then add scallops and shrimp and poach for an additional 4 minutes, or until the mussels open and the scallops are just cooked.

Remove seafood from poaching liquid and cool. Remove only 12 of the mussels from their shells and combine *all* the seafood in the vinaigrette. Refrigerate for at least 3 hours.

To serve, divide lettuce among six serving dishes. Top with tomato, cucumber and seafood which has been removed from marinade with a slotted spoon. Garnish with lemon and parsley. Serves 6.

Vinaigrette
1/4 cup olive oil
1/4 cup vegetable oil
1/4 cup red wine vinegar
1 1/2 teaspoons Dijon mustard
1 small garlic clove, crushed
1 tablespoon finely chopped onion
pinch of salt and pepper
pinch of paprika

Combine all ingredients and whisk, or process in a blender, until emulsified.

Kitchen at historic King's Landing

MUSSELS PROVENÇALE ON TOAST
The Walker Inn

You may want to double this recipe because your guests will always want more. It may be the unique way the mussels are used or it could be the wonderful flavour of the delicate Herbes de Provence. Whatever the secret, this appetizer is a winner.

50 mussels
1 cup white wine
1/4 bay leaf
1 tablespoon olive oil
1 large onion, diced
up to 8 small cloves garlic, minced
1 teaspoon flour
salt and pepper to taste
1 tablespoon fresh chopped parsley (1/2 teaspoon dried)
1/2 teaspoon Herbes de Provence *
3/4 cup dry, white wine
1/2 cup heavy cream (35% m.f.)
1 tomato, sliced and heated
4 slices of bread, toasted

Scrub and debeard the mussels, being careful to discard any that are open or have broken shells. In a large pot bring to a boil 1/4 cup of wine with bay leaf and 1 clove of garlic, minced. Add mussels and steam, covered, for 5 minutes or until they open. Discard any that do not fully open when cooked. Remove mussels from shells and reserve.

In a skillet heat olive oil and sauté onion and garlic until softened. Stir the flour into the onion mixture and add the mussels and all seasonings. Gently pour in the remaining 3/4 cup of wine and simmer for 8 to 10 minutes. Stir in the cream and heat slowly, until slightly thickened. Spoon over toast and garnish with hot tomato slices. Serves 4.

* Herbes de Provence is a delightful combination of dried thyme, rosemary, basil, savory and crushed bay leaf.

Meat Cove, N.S.

Keltic Lodge

CHARBROILED DIGBY SCALLOPS WITH CITRUS VINAIGRETTE
Keltic Lodge

Colourful, quick and tasty, these appetizers can be prepared in advance and grilled by the host at serving time. Wooden skewers will burn and should be soaked in water for thirty minutes before assembling the kebabs.

1 teaspoon soya sauce
1/4 cup olive oil
1 teaspoon balsamic or sherry vinegar
1 teaspoon lemon juice
2 teaspoons each grapefruit and orange juice
2 teaspoons each lemon, orange, and
    grapefruit zest
1 teaspoon dry pink peppercorns, crushed
salt to taste
3/4 to 1 pound fresh scallops
1/2 each red, yellow and green peppers, cut in
6 squares the size of scallops

6 mushrooms
1 lemon, cut in 6 wedges
assorted salad greens to serve 6
chopped chives

Whisk together first 8 ingredients for the vinaigrette and reserve.

Assemble kebabs, threading scallops, peppers, mushrooms and lemon wedges on skewers. Brush with vinaigrette and grill approximately 3 to 4 minutes per side.

While seafood is cooking, warm remaining vinaigrette. Arrange lettuce leaves on individual salad plates. When ready, place skewers on lettuce and drizzle with remaining vinaigrette. Serves 6.

SPINACH STRUDEL
Nemo's Restaurant

Literally translated, strudel *means "whirlwind". These famous Viennese pastries are made from wafer–thin pastry rolled around a savory or sweet filling. They derive from the Turkish baklava. Nemo's Restaurant creates a savory cheese strudel that is crisp yet melts in your mouth.*

3 cups packed spinach leaves
2/3 cup cream cheese
1/3 cup feta cheese
3 sheets filo pastry
1/4 cup butter, melted

Blanch spinach in boiling water until wilted. Drain well, squeeze out excess water and chop. In a bowl, blend together cheeses and spinach.

Lay 1 filo sheet flat, and spread 1/3 of cheese mixture along the bottom of the pastry. Roll pastry tightly, jelly roll fashion, being careful not to tear. Tuck in ends on last roll. Brush pastry with melted butter and place on a cookie sheet. Repeat procedure.

Bake in a preheated 400°F oven for 7 to 8 minutes until strudels are golden. Remove from heat, cool slightly and cut in 1 1/2-inch segments. Serves 4 as an appetizer or 2 dozen as hors d'oeuvre. This recipe was tested with "light" cream cheese.

LOBSTER STUFFED MUSHROOM CAPS
McCrady's Green Acres

Chef David Bradshaw combines garlic butter and fresh lobster to create these delightful hot mushroom treats.

1/4 cup butter
2 garlic cloves, crushed
20 small mushroom caps, stems removed
3 tablespoons diced onion
1 cup cooked lobster
mozzarella cheese, grated

Combine butter and crushed garlic cloves to make garlic butter. In a skillet, sauté mushroom caps and onion in garlic butter until mushrooms are softened. Remove mushroom caps to escargot dishes. Add lobster to skillet and heat through. Place a piece of lobster in each mushroom. Cover mushrooms with any residue from skillet and top with grated mozzarella cheese. Broil in a preheated oven until the cheese is golden and bubbly. Serves 4.

SAUTÉED MUSHROOMS
The Braeside Inn

The delicate mushroom flavour is given a zip with the Tabasco in this appetizer from Pictou's Braeside Inn.

3/4 pound mushrooms,
3 to 4 tablespoons vegetable oil
1 garlic clove, minced
2 shakes of Tabasco sauce
3/4 teaspoon oregano
salt and pepper to taste
1 1/2 teaspoons lemon juice
1 1/2 tablespoons white wine
red pepper, for garnish

Quarter or halve larger mushrooms so that all pieces are a uniform size. Preheat skillet on high heat. Add oil and mushrooms and sauté for 30 seconds. Season with garlic, Tabasco, oregano, salt and pepper and continue to sauté until mushrooms are lightly browned. Add lemon juice and wine. Bring to a boil and immediately remove from heat. Serve mushrooms in small heated casserole dishes garnished with a fan of slivered red pepper. Serves 4 to 6.

Quaco Inn

DANISH BLUE CHEESECAKE IN A WALNUT CRUST WITH PORT WINE PEAR COULIS AND SPICY PEAR MINT CHUTNEY
The Inn at Bay Fortune

Chef Michael Smith's careful blending of fruits, nuts and cheeses makes this dish an extraordinary visual and flavourful treat.

12 ounces walnuts
3 large plain shredded wheat
2 tablespoons butter
8 ounces cream cheese
8 ounces blue cheese
4 eggs

Grind walnuts in a food processor. Add shredded wheat and butter and combine just until wheat breaks up. Press crust mix into an 8 inch springform pan and set in a 300°F oven for 5 minutes. Remove from oven and cool.

Cream together the cheeses until thoroughly combined. Add eggs and mix well. Pour into prepared crust and bake at 350°F until set, approximately 60 minutes. Chill.

Port Wine Pear Coulis
2 ripe pears
1/2 cup port

Remove core and seeds. Rough chop pears and simmer in port 20 minutes. Cool and purée.

Pear Mint Chutney
1 medium onion, finely diced
1/2 jalapeño pepper, chopped (or to taste)
1/4 cup cider vinegar
1/2 teaspoon ground cloves
2 ripe pears, diced
1/2 cup fresh mint leaves (tied in cheesecloth)

Simmer onion and chopped jalapeño in vinegar until soft. Add cloves and pear, simmer 5 additional minutes. Add mint and refrigerate overnight. At serving time remove mint leaves.

To serve, warm cheesecake and serve a small wedge on the pear coulis with a dollop of chutney on top. Yields 8 to 10 servings.

STUFFED MUSSELS APPETIZER
Gaston's Restaurant

Mussels are a Maritime speciality and this hors d'oeuvre can be prepared in advance, frozen, and kept on hand for a special dinner or unexpected guests.

1 cup bechamel or medium white sauce (see
    page 48)
32 medium mussels, scrubbed and debearded
1/2 cup cooked lobster meat, chopped
6 medium scallops, cooked and chopped
6 jumbo shrimp, cooked and chopped
salt and pepper, to taste
2 eggs
1 cup milk
1 cup flour
1 cup dry breadcrumbs
6 tablespoons Parmesan cheese

Prepare white sauce and chill.
    Steam mussels in small amount of water until cooked and shells open. Cool under running water discarding any that do not open. Remove and discard one half of each shell.
    Add lobster, scallops and shrimps to the white sauce and season with salt and pepper. Put a spoonful of seafood mixture on the top of each mussel in its half shell. Place mussels on a baking sheet and freeze.
    Combine egg and milk. Coat frozen mussels with flour, dip in egg wash and then in bread crumbs. Arrange mussels on a baking sheet and top with cheese. Bake at 350°F for 20 minutes or until slightly browned and bubbly. Serves 4-6.

TERIYAKI WRAP UPS
The Whitman Inn

Nancy Gurnham loves to experiment and create new food sensations. She serves these hot little appetizers along with a variety of other innovative hors d'oeuvres for special occasions.

1 tablespoon brown sugar
1 tablespoon honey
2 tablespoons soy sauce
1/4 cup water

1/4 cup sake (optional dry sherry)
1–inch piece fresh ginger, peeled and grated
3 cloves garlic, crushed
1/4 teaspoon dashi powder*
2 green onions, finely chopped
1/2 lb flank steak, cut in thin strips on the diagonal
1/2 lb scallops
1 can water chestnuts, drained

Make marinade by whisking together first nine ingredients.
    Place steak, scallops and water chestnuts in a bowl. Pour marinade over, and stir. Let stand 1 hour.
    Wrap each steak strip around 1 scallop and 1 water chestnut and secure with a toothpick. Arrange wrap-ups on a baking sheet and bake i n a preheated 350°F oven for 20 to 25 minutes or until the meat is cooked. Serve as an hors d'oeuvre.

Sold in Oriental specialty shops.

STUFFED MUSHROOM APPETIZERS
Quaco Inn

Marilyn Landry often serves guests an appetizer tray in the living room before dinner. She tells us that the stuffed mushrooms are always the first to disappear!

20 - 24 large mushrooms
1/2 cup mayonnaise
1/2 cup sour cream
garlic powder or onion powder to taste
1/2 - 11 oz. can frozen lobster, drained
paprika, for garnish

Clean mushrooms and remove stems. Chop stems, add mayonnaise, sour cream, garlic or onion powder and chopped lobster. Spoon into mushroom crowns and garnish with a dash of paprika. Serve chilled.

2 SOUPS

There is nothing more satisfying than a bowl of homemade soup and Maritime chefs have developed a number of regional specialities that will fulfill the expectations of the most discerning palates.

Soups are economical and easy to prepare. They can be served as an appetizer course or when accompanied by a salad, make an excellent luncheon choice. The thick seafood chowders which have made Maritime cooks famous are hearty enough to be served as an entrée.

When collecting these recipes we asked cooks to share their regional favourites and we were pleasantly surprised by their variety and ingenuity. Sophisticated chilled offerings, such as Gowrie House's *Chilled Melon Soup* or the *Gazpacho* served at the Captain's House of Chester, are a refreshingly different way to begin a summer meal. Keltic's *Chilled Peach Soup* adapts well to a variety of garnishes and is a delightful combination of fruity flavours.

New Brunswick produces an abundant fiddlehead crop and recipes for their use abound. *Cream of Fiddlehead Soup* from the Aylesford Inn in Campbellton best portrays the subtle flavour of this delicate fern. Summer vegetables blend nicely in creamed soups and *Asparagus Soup with Cream and Parmesan* from Cooper's Inn or *Cream of Greens Soup* from the Bright House cannot be surpassed as warm soups with delicate flavours.

Be sure to try one of our famous Maritime chowders! While every cook has a favourite chowder recipe, we suggest you try the simple *Mussel Chowder with Thyme* as prepared by the Shadow Lawn Country Inn of Rothesay, or *Seafood Chowder* from the Palliser Restaurant. The *Mussel Chowder* is characterized by its herbs, while the *Seafood Chowder* is a feast of whitefish and shellfish. The chefs suggest that as a chowder's flavour is enhanced by refrigerating overnight, these are ideal dishes to prepare a day ahead.

Gowrie House

CHILLED MELON SOUP WITH MINT
Gowrie House Country Inn

The sweet flavour of melons combined with the tang of orange and lime makes Chilled Melon Soup with Mint a hit with summertime guests. It is refreshing, delicious and easy to prepare.

1 cantaloup, peeled, seeded and cubed
1/4 Cranshaw, Santa Claus or Cassaba melon, peeled, seeded and cubed
1/2 honeydew melon, peeled, seeded and cubed
1/2 mango, peeled and cubed
1 cup fresh orange juice
3 tablespoons fresh lime juice
2 tablespoons honey
1/3 cup fresh mint leaves, coarsely chopped
1 cup seeded watermelon cut in 1/2-inch cubes
1 cup sparkling white wine
sour cream and mint leaves, as garnish

In a food processor, purée, melons (except watermelon), mango, honey, mint, orange and lime juice. Pour into a non-metal container; stir in wine and watermelon and chill for several hours or overnight. Serve cold with a dollop of sour cream and a sprig of mint. Serves 6.

BLUE MUSSEL AND SWEET POTATO CHOWDER WITH SPICY BUTTER
The Inn At Bay Fortune

The Inn at Bay Fortune's rendition of mussel chowder is far from ordinary. In fact, chef Michael Smith's creation has fresh Island mussels surrounded in a golden coloured sweet potato soup and topped with a very spicy butter. Very different — very good!

3 pounds mussels
1 cup water
2 large sweet potatoes, peeled and shredded
1 medium onion, chopped
2 large stalks celery, chopped
2 cups milk
salt and pepper to taste
1/2 cup fresh parsley, chopped

Spicy Butter
2 tablespoons heavy cream, (32% mf)
1/4 cup brown sugar
1/4 teaspoon ground cloves
1/4 teaspoon cayenne pepper
1/4 cup butter

Prepare mussels by debearding and discarding any that do not close when rinsed under cold water. In a large pot, bring water to a boil, add mussels and steam until mussels open (approximately 6 minutes). Discard any mussels that do not open. Strain mussel liquid and reserve. Remove mussels from shells and refrigerate.

   Simmer sweet potatoes, onion and celery in milk and mussel liquid for 30 minutes. (The milk will separate when cooking but will cream again when puréed.) Cool and purée in batches. This chowder is best when made one day in advance and reheated just prior to serving.

   Prepare **Spicy Butter** by bringing cream, brown sugar and spices to a simmer in a small saucepan. Slowly, whisk in butter until combined.

   To serve, add the mussels and parsley to the chowder and gently reheat. Serve in individual bowls topped with a drizzling of hot Spicy Butter. Serves 4 to 6.

Keltic Lodge

KELTIC'S CHILLED PEACH SOUP
Keltic Lodge

Everything about Keltic Lodge is spectacular. The hospitality, the scenery and this chilled version of soup. If fresh strawberries are not in season, garnish with kiwi slices or other fruits.

8 fresh peaches (or 19 ounces canned peaches
      drained)
1/4 cup fine white sugar
1 cup sweet white wine
2 cups water
pinch of cinnamon
1 cup white wine (2nd amount)
8 large strawberries, sliced for garnish

Make a cross on the top of each peach and drop into boiling water for 30 seconds and then in cool water until the skin comes off. Remove the pits and chop.

   In a medium pot combine sugar, wine, water, cinnamon and peaches. Simmer on low until peaches are soft. Pour into a food processor and purée. Press mixture through a coarse strainer. Add the 2nd amount of white wine and chill overnight. Serve with sliced strawberries as a garnish. Yields 6 to 8 servings.

Zuppa Di Pesce al Modenese (La Perla)

ZUPPA DI PESCE AL MODENESE
La Perla

Six years ago enthusiastic customers persuaded Pearl MacDougall to expand her small café. Today, this cream and tomato seafood soup, featuring fresh scallops, shrimp and mussels, is an example of the fine fare found on the extensive menu at La Perla.

5 cups fish stock*
1/4 teaspoon saffron
1/4 teaspoon fennel seeds
2 tablespoons olive oil
2 garlic cloves, crushed
2 stalks celery, finely chopped
1 leek, chopped
1/2 cup white wine
4 tomatoes, peeled and chopped
1 tablespoon fresh tarragon, chopped
   (1 teaspoon dried)
1 tablespoon fresh parsley, chopped
   (1 teaspoon dried)
1 teaspoon dried oregano
1/2 cup tomato sauce

1 pound mussels, scrubbed and debearded
1 pound white fish (cod, haddock etc.)
1/2 pound shrimp, shelled and deveined
1/4 pound scallops
4 squid, tubes cut into rings
1 carrot, cut in thin slivers with carrot peeler
2 basil leaves, chopped or a pinch of dried

Bring stock to boil and add saffron and fennel seeds. Meanwhile heat oil in a skillet and sauté garlic, celery and leeks until softened. Deglaze skillet with wine and add tomatoes and herbs. Cook for a few minutes and then add mixture to stock along with tomato sauce. Simmer 20 minutes.

Add mussels to soup and 2 minutes later add the remaining seafood and carrot slivers. Simmer for 5 minutes. Serve immediately topped with a pinch of fresh basil leaves. Serves 6.

Powdered fish stock available in most supermarkets may be substituted for pure fish stock. Follow directions on package.

GAZPACHO
The Captain's House

Though a Spanish soup, the name gazpacho is Arabic in origin and means "soaked bread". The combination of puréed vegetables, olive oil, bread and herbs served ice-cold is a great cooler on a hot summer's day.

3 slices brown or wholewheat bread, cut into
    1-inch cubes
1 1/4 cups tomato juice
2 garlic cloves, minced
1/2 cucumber, peeled and finely chopped
1 medium green pepper, seeded and finely
    chopped
1 medium red pepper, seeded and finely
    chopped
1 medium onion, finely chopped
1 1/2 pounds tomatoes, blanched, peeled,
    seeded and chopped
1/3 cup olive oil
2 tablespoons red wine vinegar
1/2 teaspoon salt
1/4 teaspoon black pepper, freshly ground
1/2 teaspoon fresh marjoram, chopped
1/2 teaspoon fresh basil, chopped
4 ice cubes

Soak bread cubes in tomato juice in a mixing bowl for 5 minutes. Add the garlic, cucumber, peppers, onion and tomatoes to the bread cubes and stir to mix thoroughly. Transfer this mixture to a food processor and purée. Add the oil, vinegar and seasoning to processor and briefly process. The soup should be the consistency of light cream. Add more tomato juice, if necessary.

    Turn soup into a deep serving bowl and place it in the refrigerator to chill for at least 1 hour. Just before serving, stir the soup well and drop in ice cubes. Serves 4.

Shadow Lawn

MUSSEL CHOWDER WITH THYME
Shadow Lawn Country Inn

Chef Frank Gallant added a little thyme to make this simple mussel chowder a gourmet's delight. Try it on a cold winter evening!

3 pounds mussels, scrubbed and debearded
1/4 cup white wine (or water)
4 medium potatoes, peeled and diced
2 onions, diced
1/4 cup butter
1/4 cup flour
4 cups milk
salt, pepper and thyme to taste

Steam prepared mussels in wine until shells open, about 5 minutes. Discard any that do not open. Take meat out of shells and reserve.

    Boil potatoes in liquid from mussels and set aside.

    In a separate saucepan, sauté onions in butter, being careful not to brown them. Add flour and cook 5 minutes, stirring constantly. Slowly whisk in milk and heat until nearly to the boiling point. Add potatoes and their liquid, then add mussels. Season to taste with salt, pepper and thyme. Serves 4 to 6.

Indian Harbour, N.S.

ASPARAGUS SOUP WITH CREAM AND PARMESAN
Cooper's Inn and Restaurant

This is a wonderful soup to prepare in late spring when the local asparagus season is at its height. We also tried this recipe using a combination of light cream (10% bf) and milk and though the result wasn't as creamy, it was lower in fat content and just as yummy!

1 pound fresh asparagus
1 leek
2 garlic cloves, minced
2 tablespoons olive oil
1/4 cup unsalted butter
2 medium potatoes, peeled and cubed
2 1/2 cups chicken stock
1 cup heavy cream (32% mf)
Parmesan cheese, grated
black pepper, freshly ground

Clean and prepare the asparagus by discarding the ends of the stalks. Remove the green top of the leek and rinse white part thoroughly, removing any grit. Slice in 1-inch lengths.

Heat oil and butter in a large saucepan and sauté leeks and garlic. Add potatoes and broth and boil until the potatoes are barely tender. Add the asparagus and cook until just done, being careful not to overcook.

Remove the asparagus with tongs, cut off and reserve the tips. Place the asparagus stock, and other vegetables in a food processor and purée. Strain the purée through a fine sieve or food mill. Add reserved asparagus tips and cream to the soup and reheat, being careful not to boil. Serve in bowls garnished with a generous grating of Parmesan cheese and black pepper. Serves 4.

THREE ONION SOUP
MacAskill's Restaurant

It is wonderful to be around when French Onion Soup is being prepared. The compulsion to have a taste is almost unbearable. MacAskill's unique version that combines three varieties of onion with a little tomato paste and a pinch of herbs is just as compelling.

2 tablespoons vegetable oil
1/2 bunch green onions, sliced thinly
3/4 pound red onions, sliced thinly
3/4 pound Spanish onions, sliced thinly
pinch of dried oregano
pinch of dried basil
1 cup dry red wine
2 tablespoons tomato paste
8 cups beef stock
croutons or sliced French bread, toasted
mozzarella cheese, grated

In a large stock pot, heat oil and sauté onions until softened, about 4 minutes. Add herbs and red wine and simmer 10 minutes. Add tomato paste and stock, cover and and simmer 45 minutes. Place soup in individual bowls, top with croutons or toasted bread and a generous layer of grated cheese. Place under broiler until cheese is brown and bubbly. Serves 6 to 8.

The Liscomb River at Liscombe Lodge

TOMATO GIN SOUP
Liscombe Lodge

Prepare this classic tomato soup a day in advance and let the flavours blend and mellow. We served it with an assortment of crackers and Brie cheese.

2 tablespoons vegetable oil
1 medium onion, diced
4 strips lean bacon diced
1 clove garlic, crushed
3/4 cup fresh mushrooms, sliced
1 1/2 teaspoon dried sweet basil
1 1/2 teaspoon dried thyme
2 cups chicken stock
3 cups tomato juice
1 pound tomatoes, blanched, peeled and seeds removed (or 19-ounce can of whole tomatoes)
dash tabasco sauce
dash Worcestershire sauce
1/4 cup gin
salt and pepper

Sauté onion, bacon and garlic in vegetable oil until bacon is cooked but not crisp. Add mushrooms, basil, thyme, stock, juice, tomatoes, tabasco, Worcestershire sauce, and gin. Season with salt and pepper and simmer 45 minutes to 1 hour on low heat. Adjust seasonings if necessary. Yields 6 servings.

SEAFOOD CHOWDER
The Palliser

Never visit the Maritimes without sampling the renowned seafood chowders! The Palliser's creamy version is filled with seafood and simply delicious.

1/4 cup butter
1/4 cup chicken bouillon powder
1/4 teaspoon white pepper
1 cup water
4 cups blend (or milk or combination of both)
2 tablespoons butter (2nd amount)
1 cup diced celery
1 cup diced onion
1 pound haddock, 1-inch cubes
3/4 pound scallops, halve if large
1/2 pound frozen lobster and juice (if using fresh lobster, retain 3/4 cup of the cooking liquid as juice)
1/2 cup flour
2 cups milk

In a large, heavy-bottomed saucepan melt butter and stir in powdered bouillon and pepper. Add water and blend and keep warm over low heat, being careful not to boil.

In a large skillet melt 2nd amount of butter; sauté celery and onion until softened. Add haddock, scallops, lobster and juice and cook until seafood is barely cooked. Transfer seafood to a saucepan.

In a bowl, slowly whisk milk into flour, beating until smooth. Pour this through a strainer into soup and heat soup until thickened and steamy. Again, be careful not to let the soup come to a boil as the milk will separate. Serves 6 to 8 generously.

COBEQUID BAY STEW
Cobequid Inn

This hearty tomato-based soup is named for the reddish-brown tidal waters of Cobequid Bay that flow near the inn.

2 pounds lean ground beef
6 cups tomato juice
1 cup stewed tomatoes with juice
1 cup sliced mushrooms (or 1 can, drained)
2 cups thinly sliced celery
2 cups thinly sliced carrots
2 cups chopped cabbage
2 onions, diced
1 teaspoon basil
1 teaspoon garlic powder
1 teaspoon Worcestershire sauce
1 bay leaf
2 teaspoons dried oregano
salt and pepper to taste

In a skillet brown the beef and then drain well to remove all excess fat. In a large soup pot combine all ingredients and stir well. Bring to a boil and then reduce heat to low and simmer for 1 to 1 1/2 hours. Adjust seasoning to taste. This soup is excellent for the cold days of fall and winter. Yields 10 large servings.

TOMATO-ZUCCHINI SOUP
Auberge le Vieux Presbytère de Bouctouche 1880

This is a wonderful summer soup! Make it when you have an abundant crop of zucchini and fresh basil is at its peak.

1/4 cup vegetable oil
1 medium onion, chopped
1 pound zucchini, chopped into 1/2-inch dice
4 cups tomato juice
1 3/4 cups chicken broth
2 1/2 teaspoons Worcestershire sauce
3/4 teaspoon salt
3/4 teaspoon sugar
dash of cayenne
1 teaspoon dried basil
fresh basil to garnish

Heat oil in a stockpot over moderate heat. Add onion and zucchini and cook until onion is soft, about 5 minutes. Add tomato juice, broth, Worcestershire sauce, salt, sugar, cayenne and basil. Bring to a boil, then reduce heat and simmer, covered, for 5 to 8 minutes to blend flavours. Garnish each serving with a sprig of fresh basil. Serves 6.

CREAM OF GREENS SOUP
The Bright House

Sometimes the simple things in life are the most treasured. This tasty soup is easy to prepare. Its colour depends on the green vegetables you choose to include.

Green Vegetable Purée
2 cups water
2 cups chicken stock
2 onions, chopped
1 large carrot, finely chopped
2 stalks celery with leaves, sliced
5 to 6 cups of any combination of chopped
    green vegetables, such as broccoli, green
    onion, zucchini, lettuce, spinach.

Put all ingredients in a large pot and bring to a boil. Simmer until all vegetables are soft. Purée in batches in a food processor and return to pot. The purée should be the consistency of

thick tomato juice and measure 8 cups. Add more stock if too thick and add powdered chicken base in a little hot water if the purée needs more flavour.

Cream Sauce
3 tablespoons butter
3 tablespoons flour
3 cups milk
1 teaspoon curry powder, or to taste
salt and pepper
1 cup sour cream (tested using low-fat)
dill weed

Melt butter in a saucepan and stir in flour forming a roux. Whisk in milk, curry powder, salt and pepper and continue stirring until sauce is bubbly and thickened. Add cream sauce to vegetable purée. Adjust seasoning and return to serving temperature. Stir in 3/4 cup of the sour cream. Serve with a dollop of the remaining sour cream and a sprinkling of dill weed. Serves 6 to 8 generous portions.

Blue mussels

CREAM OF FIDDLEHEAD SOUP
Aylesford Inn

Shirley Ayles picks her fiddleheads and grows her own herbs to prepare this classic New Brunswick soup. While not quite as good as the fresh version, you can find fiddleheads in the frozen food section of most large supermarkets, and should follow the cooking directions on the package.

1 pound fiddleheads, washed and tails trimmed
1 potato, peeled and cubed
2 cups water
3 tablespoons butter
3 tablespoons flour
4 cups milk
1/2 cup heavy cream (35% m.f.)
salt and pepper, to taste
1/4 teaspoon dried tarragon
1/2 teaspoon dried rosemary
2 teaspoons dried chervil
1 teaspoon dried parsley

Cook fiddleheads and potatoes in the water until tender. In the meantime, melt butter in a saucepan and whisk in flour. Slowly whisk in 2 cups of the milk and cook over medium heat until slightly thickened.

Reserve six fiddleheads for garnish, then place potato and fiddleheads in a blender with their cooking liquid and purée. Add sauce mixture, remaining milk, cream and spices. Return to saucepan and reheat being careful not to boil. Garnish each bowl with a whole cooked fiddlehead. Serves 6.

Waterford, N.B.

Bay of Fundy fishing weir

SEAFOOD CHOWDER
The Algonquin

And yet another wonderful Maritime seafood chowder! The Algonquin's version is very substantial — with chunks of lobster, halibut, haddock, scallops, and vegetables in a creamy base.

1 pound seafood (combination of lobster,
    salmon, halibut, scallops and shrimp)
2 cups water
1 1/2 tablespoon butter
1/4 cup each red and green pepper, diced
1/4 onion, diced
1/2 cup butter (2nd amount)
1/2 cup flour
reserved poaching liquid plus fish stock to
make 4 cups
1 cup table cream (18% m.f.)
salt and pepper to taste

Prepare fish in bite-size pieces and poach in water for 5 to 6 minutes. Drain, reserving liquid. Melt 1 1/2 tablespoons of butter in a skillet and sauté peppers and onions until tender but not brown.

Melt butter (2nd amount) in the top of a large double boiler over simmering water. Add flour, blending well. Whisk in stock and reserved poaching liquid and stir constantly until the first bubbles appear and it starts to boil. Reduce the heat and cook 30 minutes stirring frequently.

Transfer vegetables and seafood to a large pot, add sauce, cream and seasoning. Heat, but do not boil. Serves 4.

The Algonquin

Marinated Carrot Salad (The Galley)

3 SALADS

The early Romans seem to have been the originators of salads but they liked their greens served with just a sprinkling of salt. It is not surprising that the salads we have chosen for this book show more ingenuity. We bet that Julius Caesar would have preferred La Poissonnière's rendition of *Julius Caesar's Shrimp Salad* over his usual fare. In fact it is quite possibly the best Caesar salad we have ever tasted.

Many of these recipes are ample luncheon dishes. See, for example, *Potato and Mussel Salad* from Strathgartney Country Inn, featuring local Island potatoes and cultivated mussels.

In an effort to promote healthy eating, we have tested recipes using oils with lower cholesterol, such as olive and canola. Recipes calling for yoghurt, sour cream and mayonnaise we retested using low fat equivalents. We did not notice any appreciable difference in taste. Salads incorporating yoghurt include the *Cucumber Slaw* from the Shadow Lawn Country Inn and chef Don Campbell's *Tomato and Cucumber Salad*. Both are light, crisp and ideal for the health conscious.

We are sure that there will be a favourite salad for everyone in this book!

The Galley

MARINATED CARROT SALAD
The Galley

Maritime cooks have a talent for using what is available to them, especially during the long, cold winter months. This carrot salad is an excellent example and tastes great in the calorie-conscious version, using the lesser amount of sugar.

1 can tomato soup (10-ounces)
1/2 to 1 cup sugar
1/2 cup vegetable oil
3/4 cup cider vinegar
1 teaspoon prepared mustard
1 teaspoon salt
1 teaspoon freshly ground pepper
2 tablespoons fresh dill, chopped or
    2 teaspoons dry
6 cups carrot sticks, blanched but still crunchy
    to bite
1 cup celery sticks
1 cup diced onion

For salad dressing, shake first eight ingredients in a jar and pour over vegetables. Let marinate several hours. Serve on a bed of lettuce and garnish with sprigs of fresh dill. Serves 6 to 8.

HALLIBURTON SALAD WITH MANDARIN POPPY SEED DRESSING
Halliburton House Inn

At the Halliburton House Inn, this tangy salad is served on a plate of crisp salad greens, drizzled with dressing and topped with crunchy almonds.

1/4 cup chopped onion
1 1/2 teaspoons sugar
1 1/2 teaspoons Dijon mustard
1 1/2 teaspoons dry mustard
2 tablespoons cider vinegar
3/4 cup vegetable oil

1 tablespoon poppy seeds
1/2 cup drained mandarin segments
2 cups each spinach, romaine and iceberg
   lettuce
1 large carrot, in julienne strips
2 tomatoes, seeded and pulp removed and
   cut in strips
1 leek, in julienne strips
slivered almonds, toasted

Purée onion and sugar in a food processor, and
add mustards and cider vinegar. Continue
processing adding oil in a slow stream until
emulsified. Stir in poppy seeds and mandarin
segments.

   Divide greens among 4 chilled salad plates.
Arrange vegetables in concentric circles on
greens. Drizzle dressing over salad and top with
almonds. Serves 4.

CUCUMBER SLAW
Shadow Lawn Country Inn

*The Shadow Lawn is an elegant and inviting location
for receptions and dinners. Chef Frank Gallant likes
to serve this healthy slaw with fresh salmon entrées.*

1 large English cucumber
1 1/2 teaspoons salt
1 tablespoon chopped chives
1 teaspoon chopped fresh dill
1/4 cup plain skim-milk yoghurt

Cut cucumber in quarters lengthwise. Remove
seeds and grate on a medium grater. Place
cucumber in a bowl, sprinkle with salt and stir to
mix. Refrigerate 2 hours. Drain and rinse
cucumber in a sieve, removing all excess moisture.

   In a medium bowl whisk together chives, dill
and yoghurt. Stir cucumbers into yoghurt sauce.
Serves 4 to 6.

JULIUS CAESAR'S SHRIMP SALAD
La Poissonnière

*This version of the classic Caesar salad is truly fit for
an emperor. If you try only one recipe from this book,
let this be the one!*

2 egg yolks
1 clove garlic, minced
1 teaspoon Dijon mustard
1 teaspoon capers, chopped fine
6 drops Worcestershire sauce
2 drops hot pepper sauce (Tabasco)
1-inch by 1/2-inch piece smoked herring,
   chopped fine
1 cup vegetable oil
2 tablespoons vinegar
2 tablespoons fresh lemon juice
1/4 cup Parmesan cheese
salt and pepper, to taste
1 head Romaine lettuce
4 ounces fresh baby shrimp
1/2 cup croutons
6 lemon wedges, as garnish

Using a glass bowl and a wire whisk, mix yolks,
garlic, mustard, capers, Worcestershire sauce,
Tabasco and herring until it forms a paste. Slowly
add oil as you continue beating, then add vinegar,
lemon, Parmesan cheese, salt and pepper. Chill
dressing while you prepare the salad.

   Clean and wash romaine lettuce, spin dry.
Break lettuce into bite-size pieces and place in a
large salad bowl with baby shrimp and croutons.
Just before serving add enough dressing to
lightly coat lettuce and toss. Serve each portion
with a lemon wedge and extra cheese on the
side. Serves 6.

TOMATO AND CUCUMBER SALAD
Campbell House

A hint of mint gives this salad a unique flavor. Testing with low-fat yoghurt and light sour cream did not compromise the results!

1/3 English cucumber, seeded and thinly sliced
1 medium tomato, diced
1/2 cup plain yoghurt
1/3 cup sour cream
1 teaspoon concentrated mint sauce
1 tablespoon chopped parsley
pinch each of salt, white pepper and coriander
1 head Romaine lettuce
1 teaspoon chopped parsley for garnish
2 lemon wedges

Prepare cucumber and tomato and place in a bowl. Combine yoghurt, sour cream, mint sauce, chopped parsley, salt, pepper and coriander and mix until well blended. Pour over tomato and cucumber and refrigerate one hour. To serve, chop lettuce and place in bowls. Spoon chilled mixture over Romaine and garnish with parsley and lemon wedges. Four regular or two generous servings.

ALMOND AND BROCCOLI SALAD
Steamers Stop Inn

Bright reds, greens and whites make this salad an eye-appealing delight which the chef tells us improves in flavour if prepared a day in advance.

1 pound broccoli, cut into bite-size pieces
1 medium red onion, chopped
1 tomato, seeds removed chopped
1/2 cup slivered almonds, toasted*
1 small cauliflower, cut in bite-size pieces
  (optional)

Dressing
1 teaspoon white sugar
1/4 cup vegetable oil
1/4 cup white vinegar
1 tablespoon prepared mustard
1 tablespoon chopped onion

Place vegetables and almonds in a large bowl.
  Combine dressing ingredients in a food processor or blender. Pour over vegetables and marinate, stirring several times, 3 to 4 hours. Yields 4 to 6 servings.

* Toast almonds in a shallow pan in a 300°F oven for several minutes. Stir frequently until they are a pale golden colour.

CRAZY BEAN SALAD
Charlotte Lane Café and Crafts

This refreshing salad makes a delightful first course on a warm summer's day. For a variation, add small shrimp and serve as a luncheon entrée.

1 pound fresh green beans, tips removed
1 cup fresh pineapple, cut in 1/2 inch dice
2 pears, peeled and cut in 1/2 inch dice
Crazy Bean Salad Dressing, recipe follows
2 tablespoons toasted almond slivers
Lettuce leaves to serve 6

Snip tips from beans and cook until al dente, about 4 minutes. Drain beans and place in ice water to stop cooking process and preserve their bright green colour. Drain and set aside. Toss beans, pineapple and pears with enough dressing to coat and refrigerate 1/2 hour. Serve on a bed of lettuce with a sprinkling of toasted almonds.

Crazy Bean Salad Dressing
1/2 cup sour cream
3/4 cup egg based mayonnaise
1 1/2 tablespoons chopped tarragon leaves
2 tablespoons red wine vinegar
Salt and pepper, to taste

Combine all ingredients in a small bowl and chill.

Fortress Louisbourg

PASTA SALAD
Gowrie House Country Inn

This colourful and healthy cold pasta dish is a delicious way to show off really fresh vegetables.

1 pound fresh rotini pasta
1/3 cup olive oil
1 large or 2 small garlic cloves, crushed
4 cups assorted vegetables, blanched (julienne carrots, sliced zucchini, broccoli and cauliflower flowerets, snow peas, asparagus)
2 cups vegetables, unblanched (green onions, cubed celery and sweet peppers, peas)

Dressing
zest from 1 lemon (thin peel)
juice from 2 lemons (about 6 tablespoons)
1 tablespoon Dijon mustard
1 cup olive oil
freshly ground pepper to taste
salt to taste

Cook pasta in a large pot of boiling salted water, according to directions, until al dente. Drain and refresh pasta under cold water. In a large bowl combine 1/3 cup oil and garlic. Add pasta and stir to coat evenly. Set aside for at least 1 hour.

Prepare vegetables, blanching the crisper ones for one minute and refreshing under cold water to stop cooking process. Reserve vegetables in refrigerator.

Meanwhile, prepare dressing. Combine lemon zest, juice and mustard in a food processor and continue processing while slowly adding oil until dressing is emulsified. Add salt and pepper to taste.

To prepare salad, combine pasta and vegetables, pour dressing over and stir to combine well. Serve pasta at room temperature on lettuce leaves with a scattering of chopped fresh parsley.

This recipe makes a large salad. It may be halved to serve 4 to 6 but author suggests making the full recipe as the leftovers will keep for several days, refrigerated.

Bay of Fundy shore at St. Martins, N.B.

CELERY SEED DRESSING
Drury Lane Steak House

1 teaspoon dry mustard
1 teaspoon salt
scant 1/2 cup white sugar
1 teaspoon grated onion
1/3 cup + 1 tablespoon white vinegar
2 1/2 teaspoons celery seed
1 cup vegetable oil

Whisk in a bowl or process in a food processor all ingredients, except the oil. Slowly beat in oil until dressing is emulsified. Makes 1 1/2 cups dressing.

ORANGE AND ALMOND SALAD
The Palliser

The Palliser has been a Truro landmark for four generations, offering guests a "home away from home" dining experience. The addition of grated peel and orange liqueur makes this a delightful salad, and we wonder, "Was home ever this good?"

1/4 cup olive oil
1 teaspoon sugar
1 tablespoon cider vinegar
2 teaspoons grated orange peel
4 tablespoons orange juice concentrated
4 tablespoons orange liqueur
assorted iceberg and romaine lettuce leaves to serve 6
1 small can mandarin orange segments, drained
1/4 cup slivered almonds

Mix together oil, sugar, vinegar, peel, juice and liqueur. Break up lettuce leaves and place in a large bowl. Pour sauce over and lightly toss. Garnish with mandarin slices and a sprinkle of slivered almonds. Serves 6.

HERBED GREEN OLIVE SALAD
The Compass Rose Inn, N.S.

In some Mediterranean countries it is considered a great welcoming gesture to offer your guests olives.

2 cups green olives, drained and halved
4 stalks celery, chopped
1 sweet red pepper, diced
1 small red onion, diced
1 carrot, diced small
1 garlic clove, chopped fine and mixed with 1/4 teaspoon salt
2 teaspoons dried oregano
1/4 teaspoon hot red pepper flakes
2 tablespoons red wine vinegar
1/4 cup olive oil

Combine first six ingredients in a bowl and mix well. In another small bowl, whisk together remaining ingredients until well blended. Pour oil mixture over vegetables and toss, making sure all the vegetables are well coated. Refrigerate to combine flavours.

To serve, make a bed of lettuce leaves on individual salad plates and top with the olive mixture. Serves 6 to 8.

RED ONION DRESSING
The Cobequid Inn

Nancy Cleveland, owner–chef of the Cobequid Inn, says that this easy-to-prepare dressing is the perfect accompaniment to a salad of greens. Her guests are amused by the pale pink colour and rave about the flavour.

1/3 cup chopped red onion
1/3 cup white wine vinegar (can substitute with red wine vinegar)
1/3 cup sugar
1/4 teaspoon dry mustard
1/4 teaspoon salt
1 cup vegetable oil

Combine all ingredients in a blender and process until emulsified. This tart–sweet dressing is delicious on any combination of greens.

Souris, P.E.I.

COMPOSED FRUIT AND AVOCADO SALAD WITH CITRUS VINAIGRETTE
Duncreigan Country Inn of Mabou

Eleanor Mullendore's fruit salad can be served with a choice of dressings. The first is more decadent with the inclusion of salad oil. The second, Yoghurt and Orange Dressing, is for the health-conscious gourmet.

1/2 cup fresh orange juice
1/4 cup fresh grapefruit juice
1 tablespoon lemon juice
1 tablespoon honey (or to taste)
3/4 to 1 cup salad oil
lettuce leaves
grapefruit and orange segments, sliced
    avocado, cubed cantaloupe and
    strawberries to serve 6 (6 -8 cups)
poppy seeds

Combine juices and honey in a bowl and blend well. Slowly whisk in amount of oil needed to give desired thickness. Arrange lettuce on individual salad plates and top with fruit. Drizzle vinaigrette over fruit and sprinkle with poppy seeds. Serves 6.

Yoghurt and Orange Dressing
1 cup plain, low-fat yoghurt
1/4 cup frozen orange concentrate (undiluted)
1 tablespoon honey

Whisk all ingredients together until well blended. Serve with Composed Fruit Salad. Makes 1 1/4 cups.

NEW BRUNSWICK SALAD WITH BLUEBERRY BALSAMIC VINAIGRETTE
The Windsor House of St. Andrews

The vinaigrette recipe makes enough dressing for several salads and may be stored, refrigerated, up to 1 week.

Assorted baby salad greens to serve 6
1 cup fresh blueberries
1/4 cup sliced almonds, toasted*
Blue Balsamic Vinaigrette, recipe follows

Toss the baby greens with a few tablespoons of Blueberry Balsamic Vinaigrette. Divide between serving plates and sprinkle with fresh blueberries and toasted almonds.

Blueberry Balsamic Vinaigrette
1 cup wild blueberries
1/2 cup balsamic vinegar
2 tablespoons granulated sugar
1/2 teaspoon salt
1/8 teaspoon ground white pepper
1 cup canola oil

In a blender or food processor purée blueberries, vinegar, sugar, salt and pepper. With motor running pour in oil in a steady stream and process until emulsified. Chill 1 hour before serving.

* To toast almonds: Preheat oven to 350°F. Spread nuts evenly on a baking sheet and toast, shaking often, until golden.

POTATO AND MUSSEL SALAD
Strathgartney Country Inn

This is an innovative combination that uses two of Prince Edward Island's best known ingredients — fresh mussels and local potatoes.

1 1/2 to 2 pounds potatoes
3/4 cup olive oil
1/4 cup white wine vinegar
1/4 cup white wine
3 tablespoons fresh basil, chopped

Salt and freshly ground pepper, to taste
24 cultivated mussels, steamed and shucked
Fresh salad greens
8 cherry tomatoes
Edible flowers for garnish

Wash potatoes and boil until tender. Drain and let potatoes dry and begin to cool.

Meanwhile, prepare vinaigrette. Combine oil, vinegar, wine, basil, salt and pepper in a blender and process until well blended.

Peel and cut warm potatoes into 3/8-inch slices. Gently toss with half of the vinaigrette and cool to room temperature. Toss mussels with the remaining vinaigrette.

To assemble, line plates with salad greens. Add a circle of potato slices, overlapping slightly. Arrange mussels in the centre of each plate with tomatoes. Garnish with flowers. Serves 4.

HONEY MUSTARD DRESSING
The Garrison House Inn

Honey and Dijon mustard are combined to produce a sweet yet tangy flavour in this delicious creamy dressing.

3 tablespoons raspberry vinegar
1 1/2 tablespoon honey
6 tablespoons mayonnaise
1 tablespoon Dijon mustard
1 tablespoon onion, minced
1 1/2 tablespoons fresh parsley, chopped
pinch of salt
3/4 cup oil (olive, vegetable or combination)

Combine all ingredients, except oil, in a blender. Add oil in a slow stream, processing only until blended. Yields 1 1/2 cups dressing.

Inn-on-the-Lake

MILFORD HOUSE SALAD DRESSING
Milford House

Guests keep coming back to Milford House because of its tradition of keeping the tried-and-true ways. Basic recipes of comfort food, like their House Salad Dressing, have been handed down over the decades.

1 tablespoon dry mustard
1/8 teaspoon celery salt
2 teaspoons sugar
1/4 teaspoon salt
1/4 teaspoon paprika
dash of pepper
1 tablespoon Worcestershire sauce
1/4 cup ketchup
1 clove crushed garlic
1/2 cup white vinegar
1 cup vegetable oil

Combine all ingredients, except oil, in a blender. Add oil in a slow stream, processing only until blended. Yields 2 cups.

WARM SEAFOOD AND CHICKEN SALAD
Inn-on-the-Lake

The Chef at the Inn-on-the-Lake combines sliced chicken, scallops, shrimps and fruit drizzled with his unique dressing for an excellent appetizer or luncheon choice.

2 chicken breasts, boneless and skinless
2 tablespoons butter
12 scallops
12 shrimps
1/4 cup white wine
2 tablespoons lime juice
2 tablespoons thick teriyaki sauce
1 teaspoon lime zest
1/2 cup diced pineapple
1 apple, diced
2 tablespoons each red and green pepper, diced
lettuce to serve four
1/4 cup almond slivers, toasted

Cut chicken in strips and sauté in butter until almost done. Add seafood and sauté quickly. Add wine, lime juice, teriyaki sauce and zest; return to a boil and add pineapple, apple and peppers. Heat one minute and serve on a bed of lettuce. Garnish with toasted almonds. Serves 4.

4 SEAFOOD

It is not surprising to find that the cuisine of the Maritimes goes hand-in-hand with a tradition of seafood recipes. From the early days of European settlement, communities in the region have had the fishery as their cornerstone and their foundation, and, until recently, the abundance of fresh fish was a given. Haddock, salmon, lobster and scallops are just a few of the species most commonly relished in homes and restaurants. Today, it is difficult to believe that in the 1940s the children of lobster fishermen would rather have taken peanut butter sandwiches to school than those made from today's crustacean delicacy.

Maritimers love fresh seafood and visitors love to come and enjoy it with them. Unfortunately, the very source of their pleasure is at present in jeopardy with the drastic depletion of many species in the Atlantic coast fishery. We can only hope that with limitations on fishing quotas we will once again see an increase in stocks and be given a second chance to manage this valuable resource.

On a positive note, the decline in the fishery has seen the rise of consumer interest in less common species and an expansion in fish farming. The recipes we have collected from the chefs of our region reflect the diversity of seafood both wild and cultivated.

Seafood is often the quickest and easiest entrée to prepare. *Grilled Salmon with Lime Ginger and Pistachio Nut Vinaigrette* from Inverary Inn and *Haddock with Spanish Sauce* from the Bluenose Lodge require only minutes to cook the fish and slightly longer to prepare the sauces. Two recipes that can be prepared a few hours ahead of time include *Micmac Baked Haddock Fillets* from Salmon River House Country Inn and the *Inn Baked Halibut* from Amherst Shore Country Inn. Assemble, chill and remove from refrigerator 30 minutes before baking.

For an elegant presentation prepare *Cajun Spiced Salmon with Tomato Salsa and Roasted Seaweed* from Dalvay-by-the-Sea, or *Lobster Thermidor* from Candleriggs Restaurant. The extra time involved in preparation will be well worth the raves you receive from your guests.

Neils Harbour, Cape Breton, N.S.

LOBSTER SHANNON
Upper Deck Waterfront Fishery and Grill

Lobster is the most frequently requested seafood in Maritime restaurants! This recipe from Halifax's Upper Deck will be one to remember.

2 tablespoons butter
2 tablespoons flour
1 cup fish stock or reserved lobster juice
linguini or fettucini to serve 4
1/2 cup white wine
2 tablespoons lemon juice
1/4 teaspoon freshly crushed peppercorn
1 can frozen lobster meat (11.3 ounces)
1/2 cup heavy cream (35% m.f.)

Melt butter in a saucepan over low heat. Add flour, blending well. Whisk in stock. Bring to a boil, stirring until the first bubbles appear. Reduce the heat and cook 30 minutes, stirring frequently.

Prepare pasta according to package directions until *al dente*.

Mix together the wine, lemon juice, pepper and lobster in a large skillet. Quickly sauté until warmed, add sauce, heavy cream and cooked pasta. Simmer gently 3 to 4 minutes. Add salt and pepper to taste. Serves 4.

Lobster Shannon (Upper Deck Waterfront Fishery and Grill)

LOBSTER THERMIDOR
Candleriggs

This recipe makes an excellent choice for guests. It not only tastes delicious but can be prepared in advance and is impressive in its presentation.

water sufficient to boil lobsters
1 onion, chopped
1 celery stock, chopped
1 bay leaf
1 lemon, sliced
4 uncooked lobsters, 1 1/4 - 1 1/2 pounds each
2 tablespoons butter, melted
1/4 cup butter
2 tablespoons chopped chives
1/4 cup flour
2/3 cup blend (10% m.f.)
1/4 cup dry sherry
1/2 teaspoon dry mustard
salt and pepper to taste
1/2 cup soft breadcrumbs, ground fine
1/3 cup grated Swiss or Parmesan cheese
fresh parsley or dill for garnish

Pour water into a large pot and add onion, celery, bay leaf, and lemon slices. Bring to a boil and reduce heat to simmer for 10 minutes. Add lobsters and bring back to a boil. Skim off foam and simmer for 10 to 12 minutes. Remove lobsters, strain broth and reserve 1 cup.

Split lobster tails and bodies and cut lengthwise. Remove meat from tails, knuckles and claws and cut into pieces. Discard all shells except lobster bodies and tails. Clean shells under running water and brush inside and out with first amount of butter.

In a saucepan melt 1/4 cup of butter and sauté chives until tender. Stir in flour to make a roux and gradually whisk in blend and reserved broth, stirring over medium heat until thickened. Add sherry and mustard, cooking for one additional minute. Season with salt and pepper and stir in breadcrumbs and lobster chunks.

Place shells on a greased broiler pan and spoon the lobster mixture into them. Top with cheese and broil until golden and heated through, approximately 7 minutes. Garnish with fresh parsley or dill.

FRAGRANT AND TENDER SCALLOPS
The Matthew House Inn

Quickly and easily prepared, this Northern Italian version of sautéed scallops is colourful in its presentation and a delightfully flavourful dish.

2 cloves garlic, crushed
2 tablespoons chopped shallots
5 tablespoons extra virgin olive oil
salt to taste
1 pound fresh mushrooms, stems removed, and sliced thin
1/4 cup dry white wine
1 pound fresh scallops, cut in half if large
pinch dried hot red peppers
3/4 cup roasted sweet red peppers, cut into pieces*
1 cup fresh spinach, washed, dried and torn into pieces
2 tablespoons fresh basil, chopped
8 ounces linguini or spaghetti, cooked *al dente*
1/4 cup roasted pine nuts

In a heavy skillet, sauté garlic and shallots in oil until golden. Turn heat to medium and add a pinch of salt and the mushrooms. Sauté mushrooms 4 to 5 minutes, stirring occasionally and adding additional oil if needed. Stir in wine and simmer until evaporated — approximately 3 minutes. Add scallops, hot pepper, roasted red pepper, spinach and basil. Stir constantly over medium-high heat until scallops are cooked, about 4 minutes. Immediately toss with drained pasta. Garnish with sprigs of fresh basil and roasted pine nuts. Serves 4.

*Grill pepper until it is black on all sides. Place immediately in a brown paper bag until it is cooled. Peel the blackened skin and remove stocks and seeds.

Alma, N.B.

SCALLOP BUBBLY BAKE
The West Point Lighthouse

Cooks will find that this easily prepared seafood casserole, served with a delicate pasta or rice pilaf and accompanying side salad, is a well-balanced and nutritious meal.

1 pound scallops
2 tablespoons butter (for sautéing)
1/2 cup finely chopped onion
1 cup sliced mushrooms
1 cup chopped green pepper
1 cup celery, chopped
4 tablespoons butter (2nd amount)
4 tablespoons flour
1/2 teaspoon salt
2 cups milk
1/2 cup breadcrumbs
1 tablespoon butter
cheddar or Parmesan cheese, grated

Prepare scallops, cutting large ones in half. Poach scallops in boiling, salted water for 1 minute. Drain and set aside. Meanwhile, sauté onions, mushrooms, green pepper and celery in 2 tablespoons butter until onion is softened.

In a saucepan, melt 4 tablespoons butter (2nd amount) and whisk in flour and salt. Add milk, whisking constantly and cook until sauce is thickened and bubbly. Fold scallops and vegetables into the sauce and pour into a buttered 8-cup casserole. Top with breadcrumbs, dot with butter and a sprinkling of grated cheese. Bake in preheated 350°F oven for 25 to 30 minutes, until it is browned and bubbly. Serves 4.

The Manor Inn

COQUILLE ST. JACQUES
The Manor Inn

Served in individual scallop shells surrounded by potato rosettes, the Manor Inn's version of this classic French dish is attractive and simple to prepare.

1 1/2 pound fresh scallops
2 tablespoons butter
2 tablespoons lemon juice
2 green onions, sliced
6 medium mushrooms, sliced
2 tablespoons butter (2nd amount)
1/2 cup white wine
1 cup medium white sauce
salt and pepper, to taste
4 medium potatoes, boiled and whipped
1/2 cup grated mozzarella cheese
lemon wedges and parsley springs for garnish

Sauté scallops in butter about 2 minutes. Add lemon juice and remove from skillet to a bowl.
 Sauté onions and mushrooms in second amount of butter for two minutes, add wine and liquid from scallops. Bring to a boil and reduce by one third.

Prepare **white sauce** and blend into mushroom mixture; season to taste with salt and pepper.
 To serve, place scallops in four large baking shells or a shallow casserole. Pour sauce over scallops, pipe whipped potatoes around seafood and sprinkle with cheese. Broil 4 inches from heat source until bubbly and slightly browned. Yields 4 to 6 servings.

White Sauce
2 tablespoons butter
2 tablespoons flour
1 cup milk

Heat butter in a small saucepan over medium heat, whisk in flour and cook roux 2 to 3 minutes until bubbling. Add milk all at once, and cook quickly stirring constantly till mixture thickens and bubbles.

SCALLOPS VERT-PRÉS
Chez Françoise

This simple dish of tender scallops and fresh greens can be served with either rice pilaf or Duchess potatoes.

1 pound fresh scallops
1/2 cup garlic butter
1/4 cup chopped green onion or chives
1/2 cup chopped leek, white and green parts
1/2 cup dry white wine
freshly ground pepper

Melt butter in a large skillet over medium heat. Add scallops and sauté slowly, turning once. Add green onion, leek and wine, continuing to cook until scallops are just cooked and wine-vegetable mixture resembles a light sauce. Season with freshly ground pepper. Serves 4.

Chez Françoise

JUMBO SHRIMP McCRADY
McCrady's Green Acres

A hint of Pernod flavours this delightful mouth-watering dish. At McCrady's, the shrimps and colourful vegetables are served over rice.

1 1/2 to 2 pounds jumbo shrimp, shelled and deveined
2 tablespoons garlic butter
4 tablespoons Pernod
1/2 each red and green peppers, in julienne strips
1 cup of **Hollandaise sauce** page 71

Sauté prepared shrimp in garlic butter until just pink. Flambé with pernod, and set aside. Prepare Hollandaise sauce and add shrimp and julienne of peppers. Yields 4 servings.

BOMBAY SHRIMP
Nemo's Restaurant

The chef who developed this shrimp recipe told us that the vinaigrette is delicious as a dressing for a cold seafood salad!

1 tablespoon vegetable oil
1 1/2 pounds uncooked large shrimp, peeled and deveined
1/4 cup sweet mango chutney
1/4 cup white wine
1/4 cup mango purée, fresh or canned
3/4 cup Curried Almond Vinaigrette (see below)
assorted fresh fruit and lettuce leaves, for garnish
2 tablespoons mango chutney

Heat oil in a large skillet until oil forms ribbons, Add shrimp and cook 30 seconds per side or until almost done. Remove shrimp to a bowl and wipe pan with a paper towel.

Return shrimp to pan and add 1/4 cup of chutney, wine, mango purée and curried almond vinaigrette. Simmer gently, stirring until ingredients are blended and shrimp and sauce are at serving temperature. To serve, divide between four plates and garnish with lettuce, fresh fruit, such as mango, melon slices,

kiwi slices, or berries, and 1 tablespoon of chutney.

Curried Almond Vinaigrette
2/3 cup vegetable oil
4 tablespoons white vinegar
2 tablespoons crushed almonds
sprig of fresh parsley, chopped
1 teaspoon curry, or to taste
1 1/2 teaspoon onion, puréed
pinch of sugar
salt and pepper, to taste

Prepare vinaigrette by combining oil, vinegar, almonds, parsley, curry, onion and sugar in a saucepan and simmer 20 minutes, stirring occasionally. Season with salt and pepper and set aside to cool. Shake well before adding to shrimp.

MICMAC BAKED HADDOCK FILLETS
Salmon River House Country Inn

It is said that pioneers learned to bake fish from the local Indians who wrapped their catch in wet leaves with a combination of herbs, fruits and roots, then baked it in a fire. Adrien Blanchette, owner of the Salmon River House Country Inn, jokingly comments that he substitutes foil for wet leaves.

1 1/2 pounds haddock fillets
8 slices of apple
8 thin slices of onion
8 slices of lemon
8 slices of tomato
2 teaspoons butter
summer savory
salt and pepper to taste

Prepare the fillets by carefully removing bones. Cut fillets into 4 portions and place each on a large square of tinfoil. Alternate slices of apple, onion, lemon and tomato on each fillet and dot with butter. Season with a pinch of summer savory, salt and pepper.

Enclose fillets in the foil, being careful to seal all edges. Bake in a preheated 325°F oven for approximately 20 to 25 minutes, depending on the thickness of the fish. Serve by folding back the foil to form a boat that retains the juices. Serves 4.

West Dover, N.S.

HADDOCK WITH SPANISH SAUCE
Bluenose Lodge

The owners of Bluenose Lodge say that this is an excellent buffet dish as the sauce prevents the fish from drying out. If cooking for a buffet, leave the fillets whole and arrange on a large oval plate, napped with Spanish Sauce and garnished with fresh parsley.

1 pound fresh haddock fillets
1/4 cup flour
1/4 teaspoon salt
1/4 teaspoon pepper
1 tablespoon finely chopped fresh parsley
1/2 teaspoon paprika
1 tablespoon canola oil
Spanish Sauce

Remove any bones from the haddock and cut in serving-size pieces. Combine flour, salt, pepper, parsley and paprika and mix well. Dredge fish in flour. Heat oil in a skillet and quickly sauté haddock, turning once. Fish is cooked when it flakes easily and is opaque. Top haddock with Spanish Sauce. Serves 4.

Spanish Sauce
1 can tomatoes (14 ounces)
1 small onion, coarsely chopped
1 stalk celery, coarsely chopped
1 small green pepper, coarsely chopped
1 shake tabasco
1/2 teaspoon freshly ground black pepper
1 1/2 tablespoons fresh parsley, chopped

Combine all ingredients in a heavy-bottomed saucepan and cook over low heat for one hour or until thick. Break up tomatoes as the sauce simmers and stir often as it will burn easily. Yields 2 cups.

Halibut and Shitake Mushrooms Baked in Rice Paper (Tattingstone Inn)

POACHED HADDOCK BRAEMAR
Candleriggs

Candleriggs owner Jean Cochrane prepares a menu to reflect a blending of Old and New Scotland. Haddock Braemar is easy to prepare and can be served with a sauce or herbed butter. The chef serves it with rice pilaf and fresh vegetables, garnished with a julienne of carrots, scallions and black olives.

2 pounds fresh haddock fillets
6 sea scallops
6 medium shrimps, shelled and deveined

Dressing
2 cups fresh breadcrumbs, finely grated
1/4 cup finely chopped pimentos
1/4 cup finely chopped onion
1/4 cup finely chopped green pepper
1/4 cup finely chopped celery
salt and pepper
pinch of sweet basil

Slice fillets down the centre and divide into 6 portions. Grease individual ramekins with butter and line dishes with fillets. Place 1 scallop and 1 shrimp in the center of each dish and set aside. Prepare dressing by combining breadcrumbs, pimento, onion, green pepper, celery, salt, pepper and basil, and moisten with 1 teaspoon of water, if desired. Divide dressing between dishes and place on top of seafood. Cover each dish with a piece of waxed paper, and tie in place.

Pour an inch of water in an electric skillet and bring to a boil. Place ramekins in the skillet and reduce heat. Replace cover and steam cook for 12 to 14 minutes. To serve, remove waxed paper and invert onto serving plates. Serves 6.

THE INN BAKED HALIBUT
Amherst Shore Country Inn

Donna and Jim Laceby have an extensive garden at their inn on the Amherst Shore. This baked halibut entrée goes nicely with crisp, fresh spring vegetables, such as asparagus or baby carrots.

1 1/2 pounds halibut fillets
12 ounces plain cream cheese*
1 tablespoon dry onion soup mix
1 1/2 teaspoons dried tarragon
1 1/2 teaspoons Dijon style mustard
4 teaspoons blend (18% m.f.)
1 1/2 cups coarse fresh breadcrumbs
1 cup fresh parsley, finely chopped
1/2 cup grated Parmesan cheese

Place a large sheet of foil on a cookie sheet and grease generously. Place halibut fillets on foil and set aside.

Cream together the cream cheese, soup mix, tarragon, mustard and blend. Spread over top of fillets and bake in a preheated 475°F oven for 10 to 12 minutes.

Combine breadcrumbs, parsley and Parmesan cheese. Remove fish from oven and sprinkle with breadcrumb mixture. Return to oven and bake an additional 2 to 3 minutes until crumbs are browned and fish is cooked. Serves 6.

*This recipe was also tested using 'light' cream cheese and milk and the results was equally as delicious!

HALIBUT AND SHITAKE MUSHROOMS BAKED IN RICE PAPER
Tattingstone Inn

Chef Stephen Riley of Tattingstone suggests this colourful dish be served with a green vegetable, such as broccoli, and a brown and wild rice pilaf.

4 halibut fillets (5 to 6 ounces each)
2 tablespoons butter
2 ounces dried shitake mushrooms*, soaked 2 to 3 hours, drained and sliced
4 medium tomatoes, blanched, skinned, seeded and diced
1 tablespoon sweet basil or 1 teaspoon dry
4 sheets rice paper*

Melt 1 tablespoon of the butter in a skillet and sauté halibut on both sides, season with salt and pepper, set aside to cool.

Sauté prepared tomatoes, mushrooms and basil in remaining butter. Let cool.

Soak rice paper in lukewarm water until flexible, about 1 minute.

Place a sheet of rice paper on worktable. Place 1/4 of the tomato-mushroom mixture in the center, add the halibut. Fold the rice paper to form a package and place seam side down in a shallow baking dish. Prepare remaining fillets in the same manner. Bake 15 to 20 minutes, until paper is crispy.

To serve, place a rice package on each plate, top with Beurre Blanc Sauce. Serves 4.

*Shitake mushrooms and rice paper are available at specialty food stores.

Beurre Blanc Sauce
1 lemon, thinly sliced
1 tablespoon water
1/2 cup butter, melted

Sear lemon slices in a heated skillet for a few seconds. Add water and then the butter in a slow stream. Do not boil. Serve over each rice package.

Dalvay-by-the-Sea

HALIBUT WITH MUSHROOMS, TOMATOES AND ARTICHOKES
The Compass Rose Inn, N.S.

Cooks love to prepare halibut with its firm white flesh and mild flavour. The addition of mushrooms, fresh tomatoes and artichokes in this recipe give it a little extra flare.

4 halibut steaks or fillets
juice of 1 lemon
4 tablespoons butter
2 cups sliced mushrooms
4 artichoke hearts, quartered
2 cups peeled and diced tomatoes
1/3 cup parsley, chopped
1/2 cup prepared demi-glace (brown sauce)

Sprinkle halibut with lemon juice. In a skillet, heat 2 tablespoons of the butter and fry the halibut until just cooked, approximately 7 to 10 minutes depending upon thickness of fish. Fish is cooked when it flakes easily and is opaque. (Halibut may be grilled without butter.)

In a separate skillet, sauté mushrooms and artichokes in the remaining 2 tablespoons of butter. Add the tomatoes, demi-glace and parsley to the skillet and simmer for about 5 minutes. To serve, arrange halibut on plates and top with sauce. Serves 4.

SOLE ALMANDINE
Auberge Le Heron Country Inn

At the Heron Country Inn fresh seafood is readily available. However, this recipe adapts well to any frozen white-fish fillets.

1 pound fresh sole fillets
3 tablespoons butter, melted
pinch of salt, pepper, and paprika
2 tablespoons butter
1 1/2 tablespoons lemon juice
1/4 cup blanched almonds
fresh chopped parsley to garnish

Place fillets in a single layer on a well-greased baking dish. Brush fillets with melted butter. Broil approximately 4 inches from heat for 10 minutes, or until fish flakes easily. Sprinkle cooked fillets with seasonings.

Prepare sauce while fish is cooking. Melt butter in a saucepan over low heat. Add lemon juice and almonds, stirring constantly.

Pour sauce over cooked fillets and garnish with chopped parsley. Yields 4 servings.

CAJUN SPICED SALMON WITH TOMATO SALSA AND ROASTED SEAWEED
Dalvay-by-the-Sea

There may be some that say the delicate taste of Atlantic salmon is perfect and does not need additions, but the chef who created this spicy entrée assured us that creation in the kitchen and presentation at the table make all the difference.

Tomato Salsa
6 firm tomatoes, peeled, seeded and finely
    chopped
1 small Spanish onion, finely chopped
1 teaspoon each, coriander, basil, chives,
    chopped
1 teaspoon garlic, crushed
1 teaspoon Dijon mustard
3 teaspoons red wine vinegar
3 teaspoons balsamic vinegar
2 tablespoons olive oil
salt and pepper to taste

Combine tomatoes and onion in a bowl and mix well. Whisk together remaining seven ingredients until they are emulsified. Pour over tomatoes and stir well. Cover and refrigerate to let flavours combine.

Digby Pines golf course

Cajun Salmon
4 fillets of salmon or salmon steaks
1/4 to 1/2 cup Cajun spice mix*
1/4 cup clarified butter
1 sheet roasted *Nori* seaweed*, cut in thin strips

Dredge salmon fillets in the Cajun spices. Heat a heavy skillet (authors used cast-iron skillet directly on coals of barbecue) until very hot and smoking. Put salmon fillets in dry pan and add enough butter to moisten fish. Pan may flame so be careful. Quickly turn salmon to sear other side. Remove at once and place skillet in a preheated 400°F oven. Cook for approximately 5 to 7 minutes or until fish flakes and is opaque, being careful not to overcook.

To serve, place salmon on warmed plates and surround each fillet with tomato salsa. Make 4 nests with the strips of roasted seaweed and place on top of each fillet. Serves 4.

* Cajun spice mix and roasted nori seaweed are found in most Asian markets or specialty food stores.

Salmon fishing, Stewiacke River, N.S.

POACHED SALMON WITH MUSCAT
The Pines Resort Hotel

With the sweetness of the wine and orange juice, salmon takes on a distinctly delicate flavour. This dish is best served with pasta and fresh vegetables.

4 fresh salmon fillets, 6 ounces each
1/2 cup muscat sweet wine
1/2 cup fish stock
1/2 cup fresh orange juice
1/2 cup heavy cream (35% m.f.)
salt and pepper

Simmer salmon in wine, stock and orange juice until cooked, approximately 5 to 7 minutes. Remove fish to a warm plate and reserve stock.

To finish sauce, boil stock to reduce by half. Incorporate the cream and reduce by half again. Season with salt and pepper. Serves 4.

SMOKED SALMON PASTA
Liscombe Lodge

Liscombe Lodge, situated on the banks of the Liscomb River, is famous for its salmon dishes. The chefs smoke fresh salmon naturally over wood and the result is delicious.

3 tablespoons butter
1 tablespoon minced onion
1 tablespoon each, diced red and green pepper
1 garlic clove, minced
1/2 pound smoked salmon, sliced in thin strips
2 tablespoons dry white vermouth
1/2 cup heavy cream (35% m.f.)
1/4 cup fresh parsley, chopped
3/4 pound pasta of choice

In a skillet, melt butter and sauté onion, peppers and garlic until soft but not brown. Add salmon, stir and cook for one minute. Stir in vermouth, increase heat to medium and cook one minute. Stir in cream and half of the parsley and simmer a few minutes until sauce is slightly thickened.

Meanwhile, in a large pot of boiling water, cook pasta according to package directions until *al dente*. Drain pasta and toss with smoked salmon sauce. Garnish with remaining chopped parsley. Serves 4.

ITALIAN SEAFOOD CIOPPINO
Inverary Inn

The chefs at Inverary Inn use fresh local seafood and vegetables to prepare this tasty cioppino, which they serve over rice or pasta.

1/4 cup olive oil
2 tablespoons diced onion
1/4 yellow pepper, in julienne strips
1/4 green pepper, in julienne strips
2 teaspoons fresh garlic, chopped fine
1 tablespoon sugar
2 teaspoons dried oregano
1/2 teaspoon black pepper
1 bay leaf
1 1/2 pound fresh tomatoes, peeled, seeded and diced
1 1/2 cup white wine
8 shrimp, shelled and deveined
8 large scallops
16 fresh mussels
8 ounces fresh salmon fillet, in chunks
1 lobster (1 pound), cooked, shelled and cut in chunks

Heat oil in a heavy pot over medium high heat. Add onion, yellow and green peppers, garlic, sugar, oregano, pepper and bay leaf. Sauté two minutes. Add tomatoes and wine. Bring to a boil and add shrimp, scallops, mussels, salmon and lobster meat. Simmer until fish is cooked and mussel shells are open. Spoon over rice or buttered pasta. Serves 4.

Entrance to the Normaway Inn

Margaree River sport fishing

GRILLED SALMON WITH SAGE BUTTER
The Normaway Inn

Atlantic salmon grills better and has a more fragrant flavour than Pacific salmon due to its higher fat content. The tail section is better on the grill, and the mid-section for poaching.

1/2 cup onion, diced
1/2 teaspoon butter
1/2 cup fresh sage leaves
dash of salt and pepper
1/8 teaspoon lemon juice
1 cup unsalted butter, in cubes
4 to 6 salmon fillets, unskinned (4 to 6
  ounces each)

In a skillet, slowly sauté onion in butter until brown. Remove to a fine mesh strainer and drain for 1 hour. In a food processor, combine onion and sage leaves and process until leaves are chopped. Add salt, pepper, lemon juice and butter, one cube at a time and process until smooth.

Reserve 1/3 cup of sage butter for salmon and roll out remainder of butter in a tubelike fashion, on cellowrap. Roll up and seal ends. This may be frozen and portions broken off to use with fish, meats or vegetables. Makes 1 cup.

Grill salmon fillets on flesh side for approximately 6 to 7 minutes, flip over to skin side and cook 2 to 3 minutes until fish flakes easily and is opaque. To serve, remove skin from fillets and dress with sage butter. Serves 4 to 6.

Parkerhouse Inn

GRILLED SALMON WITH LIME, GINGER AND PISTACHIO NUT VINAIGRETTE
Inverary Inn

The chef tells us that the Lime, Ginger and Pistachio Nut Vinaigrette served with this salmon dish is delicious on a variety of grilled seafoods.

1/2 cup olive oil
1/4 cup white-wine vinegar
1/4 cup pistachio nuts, crushed
zest and juice of 2 limes
zest and juice of 1 orange
1 tablespoon fresh ginger, minced
1 teaspoon peppercorns
1/2 teaspoon fresh tarragon, chopped
1 teaspoon shallots, minced
1 teaspoon fresh parsley, chopped
1 teaspoon Worcestershire sauce
pinch of salt and pepper
4 to 6 salmon steaks or fillets

Combine all ingredients, except salmon, and whisk until they are emulsified. Gently warm vinaigrette while preparing salmon.

Grill salmon steaks until they flake easily and are opaque, approximately 7 to 10 minutes depending on thickness of fish. To serve, pour warm vinaigrette over salmon. Serves 4 to 6.

OFFERINGS OF THE ATLANTIC
Parkerhouse Inn

The Parkerhouse Inn in downtown Saint John is located a stone's throw from the bay. It is fitting that this house speciality should include a variety of Atlantic seafoods complimented by a smooth garlic and dill sauce.

2 cups of water
2 bay leaves
8 peppercorns
2 large sprigs of parsley
1/2 teaspoon salt
3 tablespoons white wine
4 salmon fillets, 4 ounces each
8 large scallops
16 to 20 mussels
12 jumbo shrimp, peeled and deveined
Garlic Dill Sauce

Place first 6 ingredients in a large skillet and bring to a boil. Immerse all fish in poaching liquid. Cover and let cook about 5 minutes or until mussels open and fish is tender. Remove fish to a plate and keep warm. Strain poaching liquid into a 2-cup measure and reserve for Garlic Dill Sauce.

Divide seafood between four plates and serve with Garlic Dill Sauce. Garnish with fresh dill.

Garlic Dill Sauce
1/2 cup heavy cream (35% m.f.)
1/2 teaspoon white pepper
1 teaspoon minced garlic, or to taste
1 tablespoon fresh dill, chopped
2 cups reserved poaching liquid
2 tablespoons roux formed by kneading together 2 tablespoons flour and 2 1/2 tablespoons of butter, and formed into small balls
salt to taste

Inverary Inn

Heat cream, pepper, garlic, dill and reserved poaching liquid in a heavy saucepan and bring to a boil. Reduce slightly and add roux balls one at a time until sauce has reached desired thickness. Serves 4.

ROAST SALMON WITH RED WINE, BACON AND VEGETABLE MIREPOIX
Cooper's Inn and Restaurant

At Cooper's Inn, great care is taken with food preparation. The roast salmon and sauce are examples of the chef's ingenuity and have become a house speciality.

4 strips of bacon, diced
1 carrot
1 leek
1 celery stick
4 salmon fillets, 6 ounces each
salt and pepper, to taste
1/2 cup chicken stock

1/4 cup red wine
1 teaspoon fresh thyme, chopped (1/4 teaspoon dried)
1/2 tablespoon flour
2 teaspoons unsalted butter

Preheat oven to 450°F. Fry bacon in a heavy skillet to remove fat and set aside. Make a *mirepoix* of the vegetables by finely dicing carrots, leek and celery to uniform cubes. Simmer vegetables until crisp tender and place a spoonful of vegetables on top of each fillet in an oiled baking pan. Roast in the oven until the center of the salmon is just pink, approximately 10 minutes.

While salmon is baking combine the stock, wine and thyme and bring to a boil. Reduce this by one half. Prepare a roux by kneading together the flour and butter, forming small balls. Add roux balls, one at a time to simmering sauce until it has reached the consistency of heavy cream. Add the diced bacon and serve over fillets. Serves 4.

Chicken Supreme (The Captain's House)

5 ENTRÉES

Whether you prefer wholesome meat and potato dishes or innovative pasta creations, there is something for everyone in this cookbook.

Chefs from over sixty establishments have welcomed us into their kitchens and generously shared their specialities. The following section includes a sampling of their preparations for poultry, lamb, beef and pork, together with a variety of pasta and lighter vegetarian creations.

We are often asked, "What is your favourite dish?", and "How do you choose the recipes?" We can tell you that the innkeepers and chefs usually offer what they feel best reflects the quality and style of their establishments and we have never been disappointed.

In sampling the fine fare offered throughout the Maritimes, we found many recipes suitable for family-style meals and others that could be used for elegant entertaining. We offer several ways to prepare boneless chicken breasts in this section, many suitable for a novice cook. Spring lamb, a speciality of Cape Breton and Prince Edward Island, is featured in several recipes. Since beef and pork are popular restaurant choices, a few innovative recipes have been included.

We hope that with our directions, you will have the confidence to create these dishes in your own kitchens. *Bon appetit!*

Cavendish, P.E.I.

CHICKEN SUPREME
The Captain's House

This rich Sherry Cream Sauce is usually served in a separate dish for diet-conscious diners.

4 boneless, skinless chicken breasts (6 ounces)
1/2 pound mushrooms, chopped
1/2 cup finely chopped onion
1 clove garlic, minced
2 tablespoons olive oil
salt and pepper to taste

With a very sharp knife, cut into the underside of each chicken breast to form a pocket. Reserve breasts. In a skillet, heat 1 tablespoon of the olive oil and sauté mushrooms, garlic and onion until soft. Season with salt and pepper to taste.

Stuff the mushroom mixture into the pockets of the chicken breasts and turn over. Add remaining 1 tablespoon of oil to the skillet and over moderate heat, quickly seal and brown the breasts all over. Transfer the breasts, pocket side down, to a shallow casserole and bake in a preheated 350°F oven for 20 minutes. Serve breasts with **Sherry Cream Sauce**. Serves 4.

Sherry Cream Sauce
2/3 cup heavy cream (32% m.f.)
2 tablespoons butter
2 tablespoons sweet sherry
1/2 teaspoon cornstarch dissolved in 1 teaspoon cold water
salt and pepper

Whisk cream, butter and sherry in a small saucepan over high heat.

Gradually whisk in cornstarch and stir until slightly thickened. Season with salt and pepper to taste. Makes 3/4 cup sauce.

CHICKEN BREASTS EXOTIC
Inn-on-the-Lake

The chef at the Inn-on-the-Lake suggests serving this exotic chicken dish with steamed vegetables and rice pilaf.

4 boneless chicken breasts, 6 ounces each
1/2 apple, diced
1 plum, diced
1 kiwi, diced
2/3 banana, diced
8 pieces pineapple, diced
1 1/2 tablespoons mango chutney
1 tablespoon vegetable oil for browning
1/2 cup plain yoghurt
1/4 teaspoon curry (or to taste)
dash of salt and pepper

Prepare chicken by slicing a pocket in the side of each breast being careful not to cut all the way through. Toss fruit and chutney together and divide between breast pockets. Add oil to skillet and brown breasts 3 minutes per side. Transfer to a baking dish and bake at 350°F until cooked, approximately 15 to 20 minutes.

Combine yoghurt, curry and seasoning and spoon over cooked chicken. Serves 4.

Parkerhouse Inn

CHICKEN IN FILO PASTRY
Parkerhouse Inn

This chicken entrée may take a little longer to prepare but the enjoyment it will bring your guests is worth the effort. Lobster may be substituted for shrimp in the stuffing with the same delicious results.

1/4 cup butter
2 green onions, chopped
1 garlic clove, minced
3/4 pound cooked shrimp, coarsely chopped
1 teaspoon flour
1 tablespoon white, dry vermouth
1 tablespoon brandy
1/4 cup heavy cream (32% m.f.)
4 boneless, chicken breasts (6 ounces each)
salt and pepper to season
8 sheets filo pastry
melted butter
1 cup chicken stock
1 small garlic clove, crushed
1 tablespoon cornstarch
1 tablespoon fresh parsley, chopped
white pepper to taste

Heat half the butter in a skillet and sauté green onions and garlic for 1 minute. Add shrimp and cook for 30 seconds. In a bowl, whisk flour into the vermouth. Add brandy, and cream, and stir this mixture into the skillet with the shrimp. When thickened, remove from heat and cool.

Cut a large slit in the side of each chicken breast to form a pocket, being careful not to cut through. Season inside of pockets with salt and pepper. Stuff breasts with seafood mixture. Heat remaining butter in a skillet and sauté breasts, turning carefully, until they are almost cooked. About 3 minutes each side.

Brush 2 sheets of filo pastry with melted butter and layer one on top of the other. Place breast at one end of filo, fold in sides and roll to form a package. Repeat. Place breasts on a buttered baking sheet and bake in a preheated 350°F oven for 15 minutes.

To prepare garlic sauce bring chicken stock and crushed garlic clove to a boil. Dissolve cornstarch in 1 tablespoon of water and quickly whisk into the stock. Stir until thickened, add parsley and season with pepper.

Serve chicken packages topped with garlic sauce. Serves 4.

GRILLED BREAST OF CHICKEN WITH APPLE BRANDY SAUCE
Halliburton House Inn

We are sure this succulent chicken dish will become a favourite in your recipe collection. We tested the sauce using Calvados brandy with excellent results.

1/2 regular onion, chopped
1 clove garlic, chopped
1 cup apple juice
1 1/2 cups heavy cream (32% m.f.)
1 tablespoon brandy
1/2 apple, diced
salt and pepper to taste
4 boneless, skinless chicken breasts (6 ounces each)

In saucepan over medium heat, combine onion, garlic and apple juice. Bring to a boil and reduce volume by three-quarters. Add cream and reduce volume by half. Press through a fine strainer, add brandy and apples. Adjust seasoning with salt and pepper.

Grill chicken breasts on a barbecue or electric grill, approximately 5 minutes per side, being careful not to overcook. Serve with sauce. Yields 4 servings.

LOON BAY LODGE CHICKEN VERONIQUE
Loon Bay Lodge

We asked the management of Loon Bay Lodge for a "health conscious" chicken dish. Not only does their Chicken Veronique fill the request, it is delicious.

4 chicken breasts, boneless and skinless
1 cup cracker crumbs
1/4 teaspoon black pepper
1/2 teaspoon dried tarragon
pinch of nutmeg
3 tablespoons butter
1/4 cup chopped onion
2 cups sliced mushrooms
1/2 cup chicken broth
1/2 cup white wine
2 cups seedless green grapes

Combine crumbs, pepper, tarragon and nutmeg and coat chicken breasts. Melt butter and brown chicken on both sides. Transfer to a shallow baking dish.

Add onion and mushrooms to skillet and sauté until tender. Deglaze pan with broth and wine. Pour over chicken and bake, uncovered at 375°F for 20 to 25 minutes. Add grapes to chicken and continue to bake until chicken is no longer pink in the centre, approximately 5 more minutes. Serves 4.

HEAVENLY CHICKEN
The Innlet Café

The chef tells us that the Innlet Café serves this delightful dish in individual casseroles accompanied by rice pilaf and green salad.

8 to 10 medium mushrooms, sliced
1/4 cup shallots, chopped
2 tablespoons butter, melted
1/2 cup white wine
3/4 cup water
3/4 cup heavy cream (32% m.f.)
1/2 cup sour cream
1 1/2 tablespoons soya sauce
1/4 cup butter
1/4 cup flour
1 teaspoon paprika
2 1/2 to 3 cups cooked chicken, in bite-size pieces

Prepare mushrooms and shallots and sauté in butter in a large skillet for a few minutes until wilted. Remove vegetables to a bowl and wipe pan clean. In a saucepan combine wine, water, cream, sour cream and soya sauce. Bring to a boil, reduce heat and simmer.

Melt second amount of butter (1/4 cup) in skillet, and whisk in flour and paprika. Cook roux one minute and remove from heat. Slowly add boiling wine-cream mixture, whisking constantly to prevent lumps forming. Fold in cooked chicken and vegetables. Serve immediately or reheat at 350°F for 20 to 30 minutes. Serves 4 to 6.

Lunenburg, N.S.

SICILIAN CHICKEN
Bluenose Lodge

This is a healthy, low-fat recipe that is tasty and elegant.

4 boneless chicken breasts (6 ounces each)
1/4 cup flour
1/4 teaspoon salt
1/4 teaspoon pepper
1 tablespoon fresh parsley, chopped
1/2 teaspoon paprika
1/4 teaspoon dried oregano
1 tablespoon vegetable oil (chef uses canola)
8 slices fresh orange
3/4 cup fresh orange juice
1/4 cup sweet vermouth

Make a seasoned flour by combining flour, salt, pepper, parsley, paprika and oregano. Dredge chicken breasts in the seasoned flour. Heat oil in a skillet and add breasts, sautéing on both sides until golden and almost cooked. Cover each breast with 2 slices of orange and add orange juice. Cover and cook another few minutes. Remove breasts from skillet and keep warm.

Uncover skillet and reduce liquid to about 1/3 cup. Add vermouth and reduce slightly. Serve chicken with cooked orange slices or with fresh ones, if you prefer, topped with the orange-vermouth sauce. Serves 4.

THE AMHERST SHORE CHICKEN MARQUIS
Amherst Shore Country Inn

Donna Laceby allows the first guests to reserve a table the opportunity to help prepare the evening menu. Her Chicken Marquis is an all-time favourite.

4 skinless and deboned chicken breasts (5 to 6 ounces each)
salt and pepper, to taste
2 small cloves garlic, crushed
2 cups blanched spinach
4 1/2 ounces Brie or Camembert cheese
4 slices lean bacon, partially cooked
2 tablespoons butter, melted

Remove all fat from chicken breasts, rinse and pat dry. Place breasts between two sheets of waxed paper and pound with a meat mallet until they are slightly flattened and of a uniform thickness.

Sprinkle chicken with salt and pepper. Spread garlic on each breast. Top each one with 1/2 cup spinach which has been squeezed to remove moisture, and cheese. Roll up chicken breast and wrap with bacon. Place seam side down in a shallow baking dish. Brush with melted butter and bake in a preheated 350°F oven for 45 to 50 minutes, basting several times with pan juices and melted butter. Serves 4.

Haying near Stewiacke, N.S.

CHICKEN AND PEACHES
The Palliser

We just love a dish that is easily prepared, popped in the oven and ready to eat within the hour. We served Chicken and Peaches with hot steamy rice, homebaked rolls and a crisp side salad. The memory makes our mouths water!

2 tablespoons flour
1/2 teaspoon salt
1/2 teaspoon paprika
4 to 6 chicken breasts, trimmed and skin
　　removed
1/2 cup peach jam
1/3 cup water
1/4 cup barbecue sauce
1/4 cup onions, diced
1/4 cup green pepper, diced
1 tablespoon soya sauce
1/3 cup water chestnuts, sliced
1 cup peaches, sliced

Combine flour, salt and paprika. Dredge chicken in flour mixture and lay pieces in a large shallow casserole. In a bowl, combine jam, water, barbecue sauce, onions, green pepper and soya sauce, and pour over chicken breasts. Bake, uncovered, in a preheated 350°F oven for 40 to 45 minutes, basting occasionally. Add peach slices and water chestnuts and bake for an additional 10 minutes, basting once or twice to make sure that peaches are glazed with sauce. Serves 4 to 6.

CHICKEN OSCAR
La Poissonnière Restaurant

We suggest you prepare the Hollandaise sauce for the Chicken Oscar as close to serving time as possible. This make a very attractive entrée — bright green asparagus, golden sauce, pink crab and browned breast, served with potatoes or rice.

5 tablespoons white wine vinegar
4 tablespoons water
1/2 teaspoon crushed white peppercorns
1 bay leaf
4 egg yolks
1/2 pound unsalted butter
pinch of salt and cayenne pepper
6 boneless, skinless chicken breasts, 5 ounces
    each
1 to 2 tablespoons light vegetable oil
12 asparagus spears
12 ounces crab meat, fresh or frozen

To prepare **Hollandaise Sauce**, bring vinegar, water, peppercorns and bay leaf to a boil and reduce to about 2 tablespoons. Strain into a double boiler, cool slightly and stir in yolks. Keeping the double boiler over low heat, add butter in small cubes, one at a time, stirring constantly so that each piece is completely mixed before adding the next one. Sauce will gradually thicken. Season sauce and cover with waxed paper. Avoid overheating because hollandaise will curdle. Keep warm until needed.

Pan fry chicken breasts in a light vegetable oil. Blanch fresh asparagus in boiling water, then remove and set aside. To serve, place two asparagus spears on top of cooked chicken, top with crab meat and Hollandaise sauce. Place under a broiler to reheat slightly. Serves 6.

LINGUINI MARCO POLO
Café Chianti

Any ship's cook, able to prepare this succulent dish during one of Marco Polo's long sea voyages, would have been well rewarded by the master.

2 tablespoons butter
1 garlic clove, minced

2 tablespoons fresh parsley, chopped
    (1 teaspoon dried)
1 pound deboned chicken breast, cut in 1-inch
    squares
1 small red pepper, sliced 1 1/2-inch lengths
1 cup mushrooms, sliced
1 1/2 teaspoon fresh tarragon leaves, chopped
    (1/2 teaspoon dried)
pinch of pepper
1/4 teaspoon chicken bouillon powder (or
    to taste)
1/2 cup dry white wine
3/4 cup heavy cream (35% m.f.)
1 pound fresh linguini pasta
1/4 cup Parmesan cheese, grated

In a skillet melt butter over medium-high heat and sauté garlic. Add parsley and chicken and sauté until chicken is browned. With a slotted spoon remove chicken and keep warm. Add mushrooms, red pepper, tarragon, pepper and chicken bouillon to skillet and sauté until vegetables are tender-crisp. Remove vegetables with slotted spoon and reserve with the chicken.

Add wine to deglaze the pan; add cream and reduce until slightly thickened. Return chicken and vegetables to sauce. Meanwhile, prepare the linguini according to directions until *al dente*. Pour sauce over linguini and toss to mix. Serve on dinner plates garnished with fresh Parmesan. Serves 4.

ST. MARTINS STUFFED LEG OF LAMB
St. Martins Country Inn

Fresh spring lamb is always a treat, but this stuffed and rolled version makes an attractive dish for a special occasion. For ease of preparation, we suggest you ask your butcher to debone the leg.

1 leg of lamb (3-4 pounds), deboned
1/4 cup vegetable oil
1 small onion, diced
1/2 cup diced celery
5 to 6 cups soft breadcrumbs
1/2 teaspoon poultry seasoning
1 egg, beaten
1 teaspoon salt
Dash pepper and paprika
2 tablespoons flour
2 tablespoons vegetable oil (2nd amount)
1/2 cup boiling water
1/2 cup crabapple or red currant jelly
1/4 cup lemon juice
1 teaspoon grated lemon rind

Spread deboned lamb between two pieces of waxed paper and flatten to a uniform thickness with a meat mallet.

Heat first amount of oil (1/4 cup) and sauté onion and celery until tender. Set aside to cool slightly. Combine breadcrumbs, poultry seasoning, onion, celery and beaten egg and spread evenly over meat. Roll up jelly-roll fashion and tie tightly. Combine salt, pepper, paprika and flour on a large piece of waxed paper. Rub mixture over meat roll.

Heat second amount of oil (2 tablespoons) in a roasting pan; sear roll on all sides. Place a wire rack in bottom of roasting pan, add boiling water. Roast on rack in covered pan at 350°F 1 1/2 to 2 hours. Combine jelly, lemon juice and lemon rind. Spread over meat and continue baking, uncovered, for another 30 minutes, basting frequently. Serves 6.

LAMB SKEWERS WITH RED PEPPER AND ROSEMARY BUTTER
Café Chianti

This rendition of lamb kebabs drizzled in seasoned butter has a subtle Mediterranean flavour. Prepare everything in advance and when guests arrive merely turn on the grill; presto, you have an elegant entrée.

1 pound lamb, cut in 1 1/2-inch cubes
1/2 cup olive oil
1/4 cup fresh lemon juice
dash of salt and pepper
1 teaspoon dried oregano
1/2 red onion, quartered and segmented
cherry tomatoes
1/2 cup Red Pepper and Rosemary Butter

In a bowl, whisk together oil, lemon and seasonings. Marinate lamb in oil mixture for at least 2 hours. Toss vegetables in marinade just before assembling. Thread on skewer in this order; tomato, lamb, two layers of onion, lamb and repeat until skewer is filled. Grill on a hot barbecue until meat is cooked.

Serve with melted Red Pepper and Rosemary Butter (see below) and garnish with lemon slices and a sprig of fresh rosemary. Serves 4.

Red Pepper and Rosemary Butter
1 red pepper
1 cup butter
1 teaspoon fresh rosemary (1/2 teaspoon dried)

Grill pepper until it is burnt black on all sides. Immediately place in brown paper bag until cooled. Peel blackened skin from pepper. Remove stalk and inner seeds.

Combine pepper, butter and rosemary in a food processor and blend well. Reserve 1/2 cup for skewers and spoon out remaining butter in a tubelike fashion on cellowrap. Roll up and seal ends. This may be frozen and portions broken off and melted to serve with fish and other meats. Makes 1 cup.

St. Martins Country Inn

Glenora Inn and Distillery

SPRING LAMB CHOPS
Glenora Inn and Distillery

This simple version of grilled lamb chops will become a family favourite. Take care not to overcook the meat because lamb chops are small and will grill in a few minutes.

8 loin lamb chops (3 to 4 ounces each)
1/2 cup olive oil
1 tablespoon chokecherry vinegar or raspberry
    wine vinegar
fresh rosemary, to taste

Combine oil, vinegar and rosemary in a shallow dish. Place chops in marinade and turn to coat. Marinate 1 hour and then grill on a barbecue or broiler until meat is browned on the outside and pink on the inside. Serves 4.

RACK OF LAMB PROVENÇALE
Nemo's Restaurant

"French style" racks of lamb are available in the frozen foods section of most large supermarkets. At serving time, simply slice between the bones, allowing three or four ribs per serving.

2 racks of lamb, 12 to 14 ounces each
1 tablespoon vegetable oil
salt and pepper, to taste
1/4 cup Dijon mustard
1/3 cup dry breadcrumbs
1 1/2 teaspoons each dried thyme and
rosemary, crumbled
2 tablespoons soft butter

Demi-glace
1 package Knorr demi-glace
1 cup cold water
1/4 cup red wine
1 sprig fresh rosemary or 1 teaspoon dried,
tied in a piece of cheesecloth

Cabot Trail, Cape Breton, N.S.

Heat oil in roasting pan and quickly brown lamb racks on both sides. Remove from pan and season with salt and pepper.

Spread mustard over meaty side of lamb racks. In a mixing bowl combine crumbs, thyme, rosemary and butter. Dip lamb racks in crumbs to evenly coat mustard mixture. Bake in a preheated 400°F oven for 25 to 30 minutes for pink lamb, or until desired doneness.

While racks are baking prepare demi-glace by adding package contents and rosemary to water and wine in a small saucepan. Bring to a boil over medium-high heat, stirring frequently. Reduce heat and simmer to reduce slightly, about 10 minutes. Remove rosemary and keep warm.

After racks are cooked, cover and let stand 5 minutes on a cutting board, before serving.

To serve, slice lamb between the bones and set each serving in a pool of demi-glace with preferred choice of potatoes and vegetables. Serves 4.

BEEF TIPS MADAGASCAR
Campbell House

Mango chutney, Grand Marnier liqueur, honey and a hint of curry are expertly combined to make this beef dish a memorable feast. At Campbell House it is served on basmati rice.

1 1/2 pounds beef sirloin or tenderloin
1 tablespoon vegetable oil
2 teaspoons crushed green peppercorns
1/4 cup mango chutney
1/4 cup Grand Marnier liqueur
1/4 cup liquid honey
1/4 teaspoon Madras curry powder
1/4 cup orange marmalade
1/4 cup brandy

Slice beef in strips and brown in oil on medium high heat (add more oil if necessary). Remove meat from skillet and reserve. Combine remaining ingredients, place in skillet and cook over medium heat for 5 minutes. Add reserved beef and cook until sauce is thickened, approximately 10 minutes. Serves 4.

McCrady's Green Acres

PEPPERSTEAK WITH HOLLANDAISE
McCrady's Green Acres

Truly a peppersteak with a difference, this version is topped with a golden Hollandaise and a medley of colourful sweet peppers.

4 striploin steaks (6 ounces each)
2 tablespoons black peppercorns, crushed
1 tablespoon each red, green and yellow
    peppers, julienne strips
1 teaspoon green peppercorns
1 cup Hollandaise sauce (see page 75)

Coat steaks with crushed black peppercorns.
Barbecue or broil to desired doneness.
Meanwhile add peppers and green peppercorns
to heated Hollandaise sauce. Serve steaks topped
with sauce. Serves 4.

BOEUF BOURGUIGNON
Steamers Stop Inn

Slow cooking is the key to this Boeuf Bourguignon's flavour and tenderness. We suggest you use a good quality beef and a full bodied red wine.

1 1/2 pounds beef cubed
1/4 cup flour
2 tablespoons vegetable oil
2 tablespoon butter
1 large onion, chopped
1 clove garlic, crushed
3 tablespoons flour (2nd amount)
1 cup red wine
2 cups beef broth
1 tablespoon tomato paste
1 bay leaf
1 tablespoon each of fresh thyme, parsley and
    marjoram (or 1 teaspoon each dried)
20 mushroom caps
3 large carrots cut in 1-inch rounds
4 slices bacon, diced and fried
Salt and pepper, to taste

Cut and trim beef into cubes, dust with flour. In a heavy bottomed skillet, heat vegetable oil and sear beef cubes, a few at a time, turning often. Remove to a warm platter. Add butter to skillet. Sauté onion and garlic over medium heat until golden. Remove from heat and sprinkle with second amount of flour. Return to heat and slowly stir in wine, broth, tomato paste and seasonings. Thicken slightly over medium heat, add meat, vegetables and bacon. Season with salt and pepper, cover and simmer over low heat 1 hour or until meat is tender. Serves 4.

Wood Islands Ferry Lighthouse

PORK TENDERLOIN WITH PEPPERCORN-MUSTARD CRUST AND CIDER GRAVY
Auberge le Vieux Presbytère de Bouctouche 1880

Chef de cuisine Marcelle Albert carefully plans her menu at Le Tire-bouchon — "The Corkscrew" — diningroom. Her pork tenderloin with peppercorn mustard crust and cider gravy is a hallmark recipe.

2 pork tenderloins, about 1 1/2 pounds total
2 tablespoons butter
1 tablespoon flour
1 tablespoon Dijon mustard
1/2 tablespoon each cracked black, green and
    white peppercorns
1/2 tablespoon whole mustard seeds
1 teaspoon brown sugar
1 teaspoon dried thyme, crumbled

Cider Gravy
1 cup sweet apple cider
2 tablespoons Cognac
1 1/2 tablespoons flour
1/3 cup chicken broth or stock
2 teaspoons cider vinegar
2/3 teaspoon Dijon mustard
salt and pepper

Remove all fat and tissue from tenderloins and tuck tail under so meat is of uniform thickness. Combine butter, flour, mustard, cracked peppercorns, mustard seeds, brown sugar and thyme in a bowl. Spread paste over top and sides of tenderloins and bake in a preheated 350°F oven for 35 minutes until internal temperature reaches 165°F and meat is just barely pink

inside. Transfer meat to a cutting board and tent with foil.

Place 1 1/2 tablespoons of pan drippings in a heavy saucepan and reserve. Discard remaining drippings from roasting pan and place pan over medium-low heat. Deglaze pan with cider. Boil until liquid is reduced by half, about 6 minutes; stir in Cognac and boil 1 minute longer.

Heat reserved drippings in saucepan over medium-high heat, add flour and stir until golden brown, about 2 minutes. Whisk in cider mixture from the roasting pan and stock. Simmer until thickened, stirring occasionally, about 2 minutes. Remove from heat and mix in vinegar and mustard. Season with salt and pepper.

Carve meat and serve with gravy. Serves 4.

PORK STROGANOFF
The Cobequid Inn

This dish freezes well so long as the sour cream is added after thawing.

1/2 red pepper, thin julienne strips
1/2 green pepper, thin julienne strips
3 teaspoons vegetable oil
1 pound lean pork, thinly sliced
1 medium onion, chopped
1/2 lb. fresh mushrooms, halved
1 cup beef broth
1 tablespoon tomato paste
1 teaspoon Worcestershire sauce
1 teaspoon each, salt and pepper
2 tablespoons flour mixed in 3 tablespoons
    water
3 tablespoons dry sherry or 1/4 cup dark beer
1/3 cup light sour cream

Sauté pepper strips in 1 teaspoon of vegetable oil until crisp tender, 3 to 4 minutes. Reserve peppers and wipe out pan. Brown pork and onion in remaining oil. Add mushrooms and cook an additional two minutes.

In a large kettle blend together broth, tomato paste, Worcestershire sauce, salt and pepper. Whisk in the flour mixture and bring to a boil, simmering until thickened. Add the meat mixture and simmer. Stir in peppers, sherry (or beer) and sour cream. Bring back to serving temperature, being careful not to boil. Serve over hot noodles. Serves 4.

VITELLO AL CONTIDINA
La Perla

La Perla in Dartmouth specializes in Northern Italian cuisine. Their scaloppini is one of the best veal offerings in the Maritimes.

1 1/2 pounds veal scallopini, trimmed
flour for dredging
olive oil
1/2 pound white mushrooms, sliced
1 can artichoke hearts, drained and cut into
    quarters
1/2 pound fresh asparagus, steamed
1/2 cup dry Marsala wine
1 cup heavy cream
salt and pepper to taste

Dredge veal in flour. Heat oil in a large skillet. Add veal and sauté approximately 30 seconds on each side. Remove to a warm plate. Drain any excess oil from the pan. Add mushrooms, artichokes, asparagus and veal to pan. Add Marsala and reduce volume by half. Add cream, salt and pepper. Reduce over medium heat until cream thickens slightly, about 5 minutes. Serves 4 to 6.

The Cobequid Inn

Grain silos, Shubenacadie

ROASTED PORK LOIN WITH PRUNE AND APPLE
Gowrie House Country Inn

Clifford Matthews of Gowrie House Country Inn has the ability to find and create wonderful recipes. Save this one for a special occasion — a time when you want to impress your guests.

1 tablespoon salt
1/2 teaspoon each of allspice, ground bay
    leaves and thyme
3 to 4 pounds pork loin, deboned and tied
1/4 cup olive oil
16 pitted prunes
1 cup chicken stock
1/2 cup dry white wine
2 or 3 Granny Smith apples
1/2 cup sugar
1/2 teaspoon allspice (2nd amount)
2 tablespoons butter, melted

Mix together salt, allspice, bay and thyme. Rub pork with olive oil and spices. Place in a plastic bag and refrigerate for several hours. Before preparing loin for roasting, remove it from the refrigerator and allow it to come to room temperature.

Meanwhile, prepare prune and apple garnish. Add prunes, stock and wine to a saucepan and simmer until prunes are plumped. Strain and reserve the prune juice. Peel, core and section the apples into eighths. Combine sugar and allspice and coat the apple segments. Place apples in a baking dish and drizzle with melted butter. Reserve to cook with loin.

Preheat oven to broil. Place meat in a broiler pan and cook 4 inches from heat for 12 to 14 minutes on each side. Reduce heat to 350°F. Place pork loin and dish of apples on center rack of oven and bake 25 to 30 minutes, until the internal temperature of the meat reaches 150°F and the apples are browned and soft. Reserve meat on a warm platter, cover lightly with foil.

Add the reserved prune liquid to the pan juices, and deglaze the pan over medium-high heat. Warm the prunes in a microwave oven, approximately 1 minute on high.

To serve, thinly slice pork, garnish with prunes and apple segments and drizzle pan juices over all. Serves 6.

Gnocchi Verdi (La Perla)

GNOCCHI VERDI
La Perla

This Italian delight is often served in place of potatoes or as a garnish to soups. Served with a side salad, Gnocchi Verdi makes a nutritious vegetarian meal.

4 tablespoons butter
1 1/2 pounds spinach, washed, deveined and chopped fine
3/4 cup ricotta cheese
2 eggs lightly beaten
6 tablespoons flour
3/4 cup freshly grated Parmesan cheese
1/2 teaspoon salt
1/2 teaspoon freshly ground black pepper
pinch of nutmeg
1 tablespoon butter, melted

Melt 4 tablespoons of butter in a large skillet and sauté prepared spinach until all the moisture has boiled away and spinach begins to stick to the pan. Add the ricotta and cook, stirring frequently, for a few minutes.

Transfer spinach mixture to a bowl and mix in eggs, flour, 1/4 cup of the Parmesan cheese, salt, pepper and nutmeg. Refrigerate for 30 minutes to 1 hour or until mixture is firm.

Fill a large pot with salted water, bring to a boil and reduce to simmer. Shape the dough into small balls, drop into water and boil until slightly firm to touch, about 7 minutes.

Butter a baking dish and place gnocchi in a single layer, pour over a little melted butter and remaining Parmesan cheese. Broil until the cheese browns. Serves 6.

HUGUENOT SPINACH GNOCCHI WITH COULIS DE TOMATES
Chez La Vigne

We have included two separate gnocchi recipes because of their variation. This Huguenot-style gnocchi with a tomato sauce is a full course in itself and a most tempting one at that.

3/4 cup all purpose flour
1 pinch each of salt, pepper and grated nutmeg
2 eggs, slightly beaten
1/2 cup milk
1/3 cup water
6 tablespoons unsalted butter
1 3/4 cups fresh breadcrumbs
2 tablespoons fresh parsley, finely chopped
2 tablespoons fresh chives, finely chopped
1/4 pound fresh spinach, cooked, well drained and finely chopped
1/2 cup freshly grated Parmesan cheese

In a bowl combine flour and salt, pepper and nutmeg. Quickly whisk egg, milk and water into flour to make a light dough. In a skillet, over low heat, melt 3 tablespoons of the butter, add the breadcrumbs and stir and cook until the crumbs are golden brown. Add parsley, chives and spinach to the crumbs combining well.

Mix the crumbs into the dough and set aside to rest for one hour.

Meanwhile, heat a large pot of boiling salted water. Using two tablespoons, shape the dough into balls and drop into the boiling water. When cooked, approximately 7 minutes, the gnocchi will rise to the top of the water. Remove with a slotted spoon and place in a single layer in a buttered casserole. Sprinkle gnocchi with Parmesan and the remaining 3 tablespoons of butter which has been heated and cooked to a brown stage. Bake in a preheated 400°F oven, approximately 5 to 7 minutes, until bubbly. Serve topped with Coulis de tomates. Serves 4.

Coulis de tomates
3 tablespoons heavy cream (35% m.f.)
1/2 small leek, white part cut in fine strips
1/2 onion, finely chopped
1 garlic clove, finely chopped
3 fresh basil leaves, chopped
1/2 pound ripe tomatoes, peeled, juice squeezed out and diced
salt to taste

In a small saucepan, place cream, leek, onion and basil. Cover and simmer for 10 minutes at medium heat. Add tomatoes and cook additional 5 minutes. Purée the mixture in a food processor. Add salt to taste. Pour coulis over gnocchi to serve.

The Lookoff, Annapolis Valley

MANICOTTI CRÊPES
Acton's Grill and Cafe

Accompanied by a salad, these Manicotti Crêpes are a raving success.

12 savory crêpes
1/2 pound ricotta cheese
1 cup mozzarella cheese, grated
1/2 cup Parmesan cheese, grated
2 tablespoons fresh herbs, chopped
(combination of basil, oregano, parsley and thyme) or 1 1/4 teaspoon dried combination
2 eggs
dash salt & pepper
3 cups tomato sauce (see page 7)

Prepare savory crêpes (see below) and set aside to cool. Combine remaining ingredients (except tomato sauce), blending well and chill for 1 hour.

To assemble, spread approximately 2 tablespoons of cheese filling lengthwise on each crêpe and roll up. Place crêpes, side-by-side, in a greased, ovenproof baking dish. Cover with tomato sauce and a sprinkling of Parmesan cheese.

Bake in 400°F oven for 15 to 20 minutes until manicotti has lightly "puffed". Remove from oven and let rest for 10 minutes before serving. Serves 6.

Savory Crêpes
2 eggs
1 cup milk
3/4 cup flour
2 tablespoons fresh parsley, chopped (1 1/2 teaspoon dried)
pinch of salt

Whisk together eggs and milk. Add flour and seasonings and continue beating until the batter is smooth. Rest batter for 1 hour.

Brush a non-stick skillet with a little vegetable oil and bring to a medium heat. Add enough batter to barely cover the bottom of the pan (1/4 cup) and cook for approximately 30 seconds. Flip crêpe and cook another 15 seconds. Repeat, setting crêpes aside to cool. Makes approximately 1 dozen crêpes.

Acton's Grill and Café

Pesto Stuffed Tomatoes (MacAskill's Restaurant)

6 VEGETABLES

Vegetables are an important part of meal planning and while gathering recipes for this book we often asked the chefs to suggest vegetables to accompany their dishes. Invariably, when asked to describe how they prepare each dish, they would humbly reply, "Oh, it's nothing. I just stir fry a little of this or add a little of that." The result at the restaurant is a mouth watering treat and we felt we wanted to offer recipes that even a novice cook would feel confident to try. In the end, we managed to convince a few chefs to share their vegetable recipes with us and the results are exciting!

First and foremost, it is not necessary to cook vegetables to a soggy death. Most early summer varieties are best served "crisp tender" and we suggest you try the *Vegetable Stir Fry* from Shaw's Hotel which is flavoured with a hint of sesame oil or *Grilled Vegetables* from Cooper's Inn which take on the sweet taste of rosemary and thyme while they marinate in a gentle olive oil and vermouth marinade. Both recipes are quick to prepare, appealing to the eye and very tasty.

Several recipes featured adapt well to serving from a buffet table. Look for dishes that can be prepared in an oven-to-table casserole, such as Normaway's *Vegetable Moussaka* or the delicious *Braised Cabbage* from Marshlands Inn.

Potatoes are major agricultural crops in New Brunswick and Prince Edward Island and we decided it was fitting to include a few recipes that would highlight their versatility. *Cheese Potatoes* from the Walker Inn or *Tatties and Neeps*, the old fashioned speciality from the Duncreigan Country Inn, are but two wonderful examples of this tasty inexpensive vegetable.

Choose your vegetable dishes to complement your main course. Root vegetables such as turnip and winter squash go well with roasts, while seafoods require delicately flavoured vegetables, such as fresh green beans or zucchini. Be daring and experiment by substituting some of the vegetables suggested in these recipes. We are sure you will enjoy the results.

PESTO STUFFED TOMATOES
MacAskill's Restaurant

We tested this recipe in the height of summer when the tomatoes were vine ripe and the basil was fresh in the garden. The result was aromatic and filled with summer tastes. Substitute specialty store pesto in winter, if fresh basil is not available, and you will come close to recapturing the summer.

1 cup lightly packed fresh basil
2 cloves garlic
2 teaspoons pine nuts
1/4 cup Parmesan cheese
1 tablespoon olive oil
dash of salt
grating of fresh pepper
3 small to medium tomatoes

To make pesto combine basil, garlic, pine nuts, 1 tablespoon of Parmesan cheese, olive oil, salt and pepper in a food processor and process until smooth. Reserve.

Slice off ends of tomatoes. Insert paring knife at the 'equator' of the tomato and cut in a zig-zag pattern around the circumference. Gently pull the two halves of the tomato apart and using a teaspoon, delicately remove the seeds and insides. Evenly divide the pesto among the tomato crowns and top with remaining Parmesan cheese. Bake in a preheated 350°F oven for 7 to 10 minutes, until cheese is browned. Serves 6.

CHEESE POTATOES
The Walker Inn

This easy to prepare dish offers a nice change from the traditional methods of cooking potatoes. The vegetables may be prepared in advance and assembled just before cooking.

4 large potatoes, cooked whole
mozzarella cheese slices
1/2 teaspoon each of paprika, garlic salt, parsley flakes

Peel and slice potatoes. In a lightly greased shallow casserole, arrange potatoes so that the slices are overlapping. Top potatoes with thin slices of mozzarella. Combine herbs and sprinkle over cheese. Bake in a preheated 350°F oven until the cheese is melted, approximately 7 to 10 minutes. Serves 4 to 6.

Cresthaven by the Sea Country Inn, Maitland

DUCHESS POTATOES
Chez Françoise

This dish is an excellent accompaniment to scallops or tenderloins.

4 potatoes, scrubbed (1 1/2 pounds)
2 egg yolks, beaten
1 tablespoon blend (10% m.f.)
1/4 cup Parmesan cheese
2 tablespoons butter
salt and white ground pepper, to taste
dash paprika

Boil potatoes in a large saucepan in salted water. Drain and return pot to the stove for a couple of minutes to dry the outside of the potatoes. Cool slightly and peel.

Press potatoes through a potato ricer or sieve and return to pan. Mix in egg yolks, blend, cheese and butter, and beat until potatoes are light and fluffy. Season with salt and pepper and spoon mixture into a pastry bag. Pipe potatoes onto a buttered baking dish. Sprinkle with paprika and broil, 6 inches from heat until brown. Serves 4.

ROSEMARY LYONNAISE POTATOES
Duncreigan Country Inn of Mabou

There is nothing to compare with the taste of tiny new potatoes. Sautéed in garlic and olive oil with a hint of rosemary, they make a wonderful side dish for meats and seafood. We especially enjoyed this dish served with roast lamb.

1 1/4 pounds small, new red potatoes
2 tablespoons olive oil
3/4 cup onion, finely chopped
1 clove garlic, minced
1 tablespoon fresh rosemary, chopped
   (1 teaspoon dried, crushed)
salt and pepper to taste

Clean, but do not peel potatoes. Boil them in salted water until almost cooked; drain well. In a large skillet heat oil and sauté onion, garlic and rosemary until onion is softened. Add cooked potatoes to skillet and lightly brown. Serves 6.

Covered bridge near Sussex, N.B.

DELI CARROTS
Quaco Inn

At the Quaco Inn, this dish is served as a warm vegetable. We also tested it with less sugar and served it cold as a salad, with excellent results.

3 pounds carrots, pared and cut on the bias
1 can tomato soup
1/2 cup vinegar
1 scant cup sugar
1 tablespoon Dijon style mustard
1 teaspoon Worcestershire sauce
1/2 each red and green pepper, thinly sliced
1 small onion, thinly sliced

Boil carrots in a small amount of salted water, only until crisp.

Whisk together tomato soup, vinegar, sugar, mustard and Worcestershire sauce. Add peppers and onion. Pour sauce over carrots and serve either warm or cold. Serves 6-8.

TATTIES AND NEEPS (POTATOES AND TURNIPS)
Duncreigan Country Inn of Mabou

Tatties and Neeps are a wonderful addition to a roast or meat dish. They can be prepared early in the day and reheated at serving time. Variations of this traditional Mabou recipe include using carrots in place of turnips or adding cheese to the neeps.

1 small turnip, peeled and cubed
1 medium onion, diced
4 large potatoes, peeled and quartered
1/4 cup butter
salt and pepper, to taste

Boil turnip and onion in a small saucepan until tender. Drain, reserving cooking liquid. Boil potatoes in a separate saucepan until tender. Drain, then dry potatoes over low heat, breaking up with a fork to allow steam to escape. Mash potatoes and gradually add butter and 1 teaspoon of cooking water to make a stiff mashed potato. Season with salt and pepper and cool slightly.

Quaco Inn

Place reserved turnip and onion in a food processor and purée. Blend into potatoes and place in a piping bag with a large star tip. Pipe onto a cookie sheet that has been lined with greased waxed paper. Chill uncovered, until firm.

To serve, place on a cookie sheet and reheat at 350°F for about 20 minutes. Serves 6 to 8.

GRILLED VEGETABLES
Cooper's Inn and Restaurant

We found this vegetable recipe to be one of the easiest and tastiest in our book. You are not limited to the vegetables listed in our ingredients and may substitute any seasonal fare that grills well.

4 to 6 cups of summer vegetables, cut in
    portions suitable for grilling (zucchini,
    pattypan squash cubes, sweet pepper
    squares, whole mushrooms etc.)
1/3 cup olive oil
3 tablespoons lemon juice
3 tablespoons dry white vermouth
1 tablespoon ground rosemary
1 1/2 teaspoon dried thyme
1/4 teaspoon salt
1/4 teaspoon sugar
freshly ground pepper

Prepare vegetables. In a bowl whisk together remaining ingredients until well combined. Marinate vegetables in oil mixture for at least 30 minutes. Heat a grill or barbecue and place in a grilling basket and cook for 5 minutes on each side until browned and cooked through.

Marinade is sufficient for 4 to 6 cups of prepared vegetables. Allow 1 cup of prepared vegetables per serving. Serves 4 to 6.

Shaw's Hotel

VEGETABLE MEDLEY STIR FRY
Shaw's Hotel

A hint of sesame turns this vegetable medley into a gourmet's delight! Experiment with different vegetables, but be sure that they require about the same cooking time.

1 tablespoon vegetable oil
1 medium onion, cut in wedges
1 clove garlic, minced
1 cup broccoli flowerets
1 cup cauliflower flowerets
1 small zucchini, sliced
1 tablespoon soya sauce
1 teaspoon lemon pepper
1/2 teaspoon sesame oil
2 small tomatoes, cut in wedges
1 tablespoon sesame seeds, toasted

Heat oil in a wok or large skillet over medium heat. Add onion and garlic, stir fry until onion starts to soften. Add broccoli and cauliflower and stir fry about 2 minutes. Add zucchini and cook an additional 2 minutes, until crisp tender. Stir in soya sauce, lemon pepper and sesame oil. Add tomato wedges and cook one minute. Sprinkle with toasted sesame seeds. Serves 4 to 6.

The Normaway Inn

VEGETABLE MOUSSAKA
The Normaway Inn

This recipe may take a little longer to prepare but the time is well worth the effort. With its aromatic Mediterranean flavour we found it a delicious accompaniment for grilled seafood and meats. You might want to garnish Vegetable Moussaka with black olives and serve with hot garlic bread to make an ample luncheon dish.

1 medium eggplant
1 1/2 tablespoons coarse salt
1/4 cup olive oil
2 8-inch zucchinis
1 cup ricotta or cottage cheese
1/2 cup Parmesan cheese
3 eggs, lightly beaten
1/2 cup heavy cream (35% m.f.)
1/2 teaspoon dried oregano
dash of salt and pepper
1/2 cup peeled, chopped tomatoes
2 large or 3 medium tomatoes, sliced

Cut eggplant into slices 1/3-inch thick. Sprinkle with salt and layer in a colander. Place a heavy weight on top and let stand for 2 hours to let the bitterness drain out. Rinse well under cold water and then dry, squeezing out excess water with paper towels. Brush slices with olive oil and bake in a preheated 350°F oven, turning once, until golden, approximately 20 minutes. Reserve.

Slice zucchini on a bias, 1/4-inch thick. Brush with olive oil and bake in a preheated 425°F oven, turning once, until golden, approximately 5 minutes. Reserve.

In a bowl combine cheeses, eggs, cream and seasonings and blend well.

To assemble moussaka, lightly grease an 8-cup casserole dish and place chopped tomatoes in bottom. Arrange a layer each of eggplant, zucchini and sliced tomatoes. Repeat with three more layers. Pour egg mixture over vegetables shaking casserole to distribute custard through layers. Bake in a preheated 325°F oven for 1 hour or until set and golden. Remove from oven and rest for 10 minutes.

Serve as a vegetable with meat or seafood entreés or as an appetizer on tomato sauce garnished with black olives. Serves 4 to 6 as an appetizer or 8 generously as a vegetable.

Halifax Farmers' Market

ZUCCHINI BASIL PANCAKES
Duncreigan Country Inn of Mabou

Eleanor Mullendore of Duncreigan Country Inn says that this is a good use for all those surplus zucchini at the end of the summer!

3 cups grated zucchini
salt to season
1 egg
1/4 cup milk
1/4 teaspoon hot sauce (e.g. Tabasco)
freshly ground pepper, to taste
2 tablespoons basil and/or parsley, finely chopped
1/2 cup flour
1/4 cup grated Parmesan cheese
1 1/2 teaspoons baking powder

Peel, remove seeds and grate zucchini. Lightly salt the zucchini and place in a colander covered with a weighted plate; let stand 30 minutes and then squeeze out excess liquid.

In a bowl, beat together, egg, milk, hot sauce, pepper to taste and herbs. Add zucchini to egg mixture, stirring to combine. Mix together flour, cheese and baking powder and add to the egg mixture, stirring well. Preheat a greased skillet to 400°F. Spoon 3 to 4 tablespoons of batter on skillet and cook about 3 minutes on one side, until brown; flip and cook 1 minute more. Top with butter as and serve as a side dish for entrées. Serves 6.

Marshlands Inn

VEGETARIAN ZUCCHINI BAKE
Salmon River House Country Inn

This is a great dish to prepare when zucchini and tomatoes are overflowing in your garden. Tasty and flavourful, it is a good choice to accompany meat and seafood.

4 small or 3 medium-sized zucchinis
2 tablespoons butter
1 garlic clove, crushed
1 small onion, diced
4 medium tomatoes, diced 1/4-inch cubes
1 teaspoon each of sweet basil and oregano
salt and pepper to taste
1/4 cup grated Parmesan cheese
1/2 cup mozzarella cheese, grated
buttered breadcrumbs

Slice the zucchini on the bias into 1/4-inch slices. In a skillet, melt butter. Add garlic, then zucchini and sauté until it is browned and slightly transparent. Remove zucchini and reserve. Add onion, tomatoes and seasoning to skillet and sauté for a few minutes until vegetables are softened.

Grease 4 oven-proof au-gratin dishes or an 8-cup casserole and layer zucchini, a sprinkling of Parmesan, a layer of tomatoes and another sprinkling of Parmesan. Repeat layers, ending with tomatoes and Parmesan. Cover layers with grated mozzarella and breadcrumbs. Bake in a preheated 350°F oven for 30 minutes until golden and bubbly. Serves 4.

BRAISED RED CABBAGE
Marshlands Inn

A hearty, flavourful dish, Marshlands' Braised Red Cabbage is delicious with pork and an innovative addition to a buffet table.

1/2 cup white vinegar
1/3 cup sugar
3/4 teaspoon nutmeg
2 apples, diced
red cabbage, shredded (about 1 1/4 pounds)

In a saucepan whisk together vinegar, sugar and nutmeg and cook over medium high heat until sugar is dissolved. Add apple and cabbage and simmer, covered, for 45 minutes. Drain excess liquid. Serves 6.

HARVARD BEETS
Marshlands Inn

While freshly cooked beets are preferred, this recipe transforms canned beets into a colorful and flavourful dish suitable for Guests.

2 cups sliced cooked beets (19-ounce can sliced beets)
1/4 cup cooking liquid
1/4 cup vinegar
4 teaspoons cornstarch
1 tablespoon vegetable oil
1/2 cup sugar

Combine beet liquid, vinegar, cornstarch, oil and sugar. Bring to a boil stirring frequently. Add beets to sauce and return to serving temperature. Serves 4.

TOMATO CHUTNEY
Liscombe Lodge

The inclusion of maple syrup in this chutney recipe gives it a unique sweet, yet tart, flavour. This condiment's great taste and pretty colour makes it a fitting addition to seafood, poultry and pork dishes.

Partridge berries

2 1/2 pounds ripe, tomatoes, peeled and diced
2 pounds tart apples, peeled, cored and sliced
1 1/4 cups sugar
3/4 cup maple syrup
2/3 cup cider vinegar
1 teaspoon mixed pickling spices
1/2 teaspoon whole cloves

Place tomatoes in a bowl, cover and put a heavy weight on top. Press overnight and in the morning, pour off juice. Transfer tomatoes to a large saucepan and add apples, sugar, maple syrup and vinegar. Tie up spices in a cheesecloth bag and add to the saucepan. Bring to a boil and simmer until thick, about 1 1/2 hours. Remove the spice bag. Pour chutney into hot sterilized jars and seal. Yields approximately 6 cups.

7 DESSERTS

The dilemma of desserts! In this day and age when we are constantly warned to control our calorie and fat intake, and told to be more physically active in our drive to perfect ourselves, how can we possibly dive into a rich dessert with any conscience at all. We certainly don't want to become sweet sneaks scurrying off to a dark closet to eat creamy éclairs, nor do we want to become cynics who ridicule and scorn the enjoyment of food.

The only solution we arrived at, while still including a dessert section in our book, was to cry out "Moderation!" Life in moderation seems to be the most reasonable route to follow. With this in mind, we went in search of delectable desserts from the chefs of our Maritime restaurants asking them to share a sampling of decadent, semi-decadent and downright healthy recipes. They did not disappoint us.

As dessert is the finale to dinner, it should be in harmony with other courses of the meal, drawing it to a comfortable close. If you have served a rich main course, you may want to serve a light dessert, or conversely, if your entrée had little protein, a dessert made with milk or cheese will compliment the meal.

Summer dining begs for cool desserts and those that feature the bounty of our orchards and gardens. We recommend the fruit pie recipes or parfait-style dishes included in our desserts. During the cold days of winter, hot and hearty meals are in order and lend themselves to steamy puddings and warm cakes.

Be adventuresome and prepare some of these delicious desserts. Decide to go healthy or completely decadent — the choice is yours. Enjoy!

Salmon River House Country Inn

BANANA ROYALE
The Galley

We like to serve desserts that can be prepared in advance, leaving the hostess time to enjoy her guests. This recipe fills the bill.

3 tablespoons sugar (for syrup)
1/3 cup water
dark rum
2 tablespoons butter
1/2 cup brown sugar
1/4 teaspoon cinnamon
1/4 teaspoon nutmeg
1/4 cup blend
3 bananas, sliced
vanilla ice cream
whipped cream and fresh mint leaves to
    garnish, if desired

For rum syrup, combine 3 tablespoons sugar and water in a small saucepan and bring to a boil. Cook until sugar is dissolved and set aside to cool. Add an equal amount of dark rum to syrup and refrigerate.

For sauce, melt butter in a saucepan and stir in sugar, cinnamon, nutmeg, and blend. Whisk sauce and simmer until slightly thickened, about 5 minutes. Cool and store.

Before serving, heat butter sauce with sliced bananas. Place a scoop of ice cream in six serving dishes, top with banana sauce mixture and 2 tablespoons of rum syrup. Decorate with whipped cream and fresh mint leaves, if desired. Serves 6.

Ross Farm Museum, near Campbell House

FRESH FRUIT YOGHURT PARFAIT
Salmon River House Country Inn

Don't save this simple creation for dessert only. It is an excellent early morning starter or refreshing lunchtime meal.

2 to 3 cups fresh fruit of choice (orange, peach, pineapple, strawberry, raspberry etc.)
lemon juice
2 cups low-fat vanilla or natural yoghurt

Prepare fruit and chop. You may use one, two or several different kinds of fruit, depending on what is in season. Sprinkle with lemon juice to preserve colour. In a tall parfait or wine glass, place a spoonful of yoghurt followed by a spoonful of fruit. Alternate fruit and yoghurt to fill the glass; finish with yoghurt and top with a fresh berry or maraschino cherry. Serves 4.

CREAM CROWDIE
Campbell House

In Cream Crowdie, rolled oats and Drambuie reflect the strength of Scottish influence in Nova Scotian cooking.

3 tablespoons oatmeal
1 cup heavy cream (35% m.f.)
1 ounce Drambuie liqueur
1 tablespoon sugar
vanilla ice cream

Spread oatmeal evenly on a baking sheet and bake at 350°F for 10 minutes, until golden brown. Remove from oven and cool. Place cream in a chilled bowl and whip until stiff. Add cooled oatmeal, Drambuie and sugar. Place ice cream in a champagne glass, top with oatmeal-cream mixture. Serves 4 to 6.

Dutch Appel Taart (The Blomidon Inn)

DUTCH APPEL TAART
The Blomidon Inn

At the Blomidon Inn, only Annapolis Valley Red Delicious apples are used for this wonderful tart. We're sure that you won't compromise the results if you choose another variety of apple, but don't alter the sugar or the spices. They serve it garnished with whipped cream and toasted almond slices.

1 cup butter
2 cups flour
1 cup sugar
1 teaspoon baking powder
1 large egg, beaten
3 pounds Red Delicious apples, peeled and
    cored and diced in 1/4-inch pieces
1 tablespoon lemon juice
1 cup sugar
2 teaspoons nutmeg
2 tablespoons cinnamon
Pinch of cloves
3 tablespoons sherry

In a large mixing bowl, cut together butter, flour, sugar and baking powder. Incorporate beaten egg. While this crust mixture is still coarse and crumbly, reserve 1/2 cup for topping. Mix remainder into a ball press gently over the bottom and half way up the side of a greased and floured 10-inch springform pan. The dough should be of uniform thickness, just over 1/4 inch.

Mix together the prepared apples, lemon juice, sugar, spices and flavouring and place on the crust. The level of filling will exceed the height of the crust, but baking will compensate. Sprinkle with reserved topping and bake on the middle rack in a preheated oven at 375°F until top is a rich golden brown, approximately 1 hour. After baking, allow the *taart* to cool and then refrigerate. Unmold from springform pan and divide into 12 servings.

APPLE PIE
The Manor Inn

An apple pie to make Mum proud! We tested the Manor Inn's version with early Gravenstein apples with excellent results.

Pastry
1 3/4 cups flour
3/4 teaspoon salt
3/4 cup lard or shortening
4 - 5 tablespoons cold water

Combine flour and salt in a mixing bowl. Cut in shortening or lard with a pastry blender until mixture is the size of large peas. Sprinkle water on the dough, a little at a time, and blend it in lightly. Form the dough into a ball, handling it as little as possible.

Use a lightly floured surface, preferably with a pastry cloth and a covered rolling pin. Divide pastry into two and form each half into a flattened ball. Roll lightly from the centre until the pastry is about 1 inch larger than pie plate.

Roll pastry over rolling pin and transfer to a greased pie plate. Unroll and ease into place, being careful not to stretch the pastry. Trim off any excess.

Filling
4 cups peeled, cored and sliced apples
1 cup sugar
1/4 cup flour
1 teaspoon cinnamon
1/2 teaspoon nutmeg

Toss all ingredients together in a bowl. Place in unbaked pie shell. Cover with top crust and bake at 375°F for 35 to 40 minutes, until browned. Cool on a rack and refrigerate until ready to serve. Serves 6 to 8.

BLUEBERRY LEMON PIE
The Compass Rose, N.B.

Put this recipe in your file of "special occasion" desserts. The blueberry-lemon combination is delightful and the pie can be made any time using frozen berries.

1 large pie shell, prebaked and cooled
3 egg yolks
1 can Eagle Brand sweetened condensed milk
1/2 cup lemon juice
1 tablespoon lemon zest
4 cups blueberries
1/2 cup liquid honey
1/2 cup water
2 tablespoons cornstarch
2 teaspoons lemon juice
1 cup heavy cream (35% m.f.)
1/4 teaspoon almond extract
2 tablespoons liquid honey
1/4 cup toasted almond slivers

In a medium-sized bowl, beat together egg yolks, sweetened condensed milk, lemon juice and lemon zest. Pour into prepared pie crust and bake in a 350°F oven for 10 minutes. Remove from oven and let cool.

In a saucepan, combine 1 cup of blueberries, honey, water and cornstarch. Bring to boiling point and let simmer until thickened. Remove from heat and stir in lemon juice. Cool thoroughly and stir in 3 cups of blueberries. Spoon into pie shell over lemon mixture and refrigerate.

At serving time, whip cream, sweeten with honey and add almond flavoring. Spoon onto pie and sprinkle with almonds. Serves 6 to 8.

Blueberry picking

RASPBERRY PIE
Drury Lane Steak House

The addition of orange juice adds extra tartness to this fruit pie which can be counteracted with a good dollop of whipping cream.

Pastry to make one 9-inch double crust pie
   (see page 102)
5 cups raspberries, fresh or frozen
1 tablespoon orange juice
1 cup sugar
1/3 cup flour
1/2 teaspoon salt

Mix together raspberries, orange juice, sugar, flour and salt. Line a pie plate with pastry, fill with berry mixture and cover with second piece of pastry. Flute edges, sprinkle crust with water and shake a small amount of sugar over the pie. Bake in a preheated 400°F oven 40 to 50 minutes. Serves 6 to 8.

BUMBLE BERRY PIE
Inverary Inn

The chef at the Inverary Inn tells us that you can use any combination of fruit in Bumble Berry Pie, but you may have to adjust the sugar.

1/2 cup blueberries
1/2 cup strawberries, quartered
1/2 cup raspberries
1/2 cup blackberries
1/2 cup apples, finely sliced
1/2-3/4 cup sugar
1 tablespoon cornstarch
1/4 teaspoon cinnamon

Prepare a pastry of your choice to make a 9-inch pie. Mix together all ingredients and place in unbaked pie crust. Cover with pastry and bake at 350°F until golden brown, approximately 40 to 45 minutes.

RUM RUNNER PIE
The Matthew House Inn

Stories of the prohibition era and bootlegging on the Island abound, embellished, it seems, with every passing year! This recipe works best with a crumb crust, although a baked crust can be used. Prepare the crust ahead and chill it while making the filling.

Crust
2/3 cup graham cracker crumbs
2/3 cup finely ground hazelnuts
3 tablespoons sugar
1/3 cup butter, melted

Filling
1/3 cup cold water
1 envelope unflavored gelatin
2/3 cup sugar
4 egg yolks
1/4 cup dark rum (not spiced)
1 cup heavy cream (35% m.f.)

Garnish
1/3 cup heavy cream, whipped
Fresh fruit such as raspberries, strawberries
    or kiwi
Reserved hazelnuts

To prepare crust, combine dry ingredients, reserving 1 tablespoon of hazelnuts for garnish. Mix in butter, tossing to coat. Press over the bottom and up the sides of a 9-inch pie plate and bake at 350°F for 8 to 9 minutes. Cool, then chill.

For the filling, add gelatin to cold water in a small saucepan. Stir constantly over low heat, then medium heat to dissolve. In a separate bowl, beat sugar and egg yolks. Stir in hot gelatin. Slowly add rum, beating constantly.

In a chilled bowl, whip the cream into stiff peaks and then fold into the gelatin mixture. Set the bowl into a basin of crushed ice and whip until thick and starting to set, 7 to 10 minutes. Scoop into chilled pie shell. Cover with plastic wrap and chill 6 hours or overnight.

Garnish with freshly whipped cream and fresh fruit. Sprinkle with finely chopped hazelnuts.

At the Matthew House, this dessert is served with espresso. Serves 6.

BUTTERSCOTCH PIE
Steamers Stop Inn

This recipe makes a large, tall butterscotch pie. We are sure it will become a family favourite.

4 cups milk
2 cups brown sugar
1/4 cup butter
1/2 cup cornstarch
pinch of salt
2 eggs
1 teaspoon vanilla
1 deep 9-inch pie shell, baked and cooled
1 cup heavy cream (35% m.f.)

In a large saucepan over medium heat, bring 4 cups of milk, brown sugar and butter to a boil, stirring constantly.

In a bowl combine cornstarch, salt, 1/2 cup of the hot milk and eggs. Stir into hot milk mixture. Simmer until thickened. Remove from heat and stir in vanilla. Pour into pie shell. Chill. Serve with whipped cream. Yields 6 to 8 servings.

Saint John River near Gagetown, N.B.

Lemon Almond Tart (Acton's Grill and Café)

LEMON ALMOND TART
Acton's Grill and Café

We found the sharp lemon flavour of this tart a nice alternative to the sweetness of most desserts.

1 cup flour
3 1/2 tablespoons sugar
1/3 cup butter, softened
4 eggs
1/2 cup sugar (2nd amount)
zest of 1 1/2 lemons (thinly shaved rind)
1/2 cup lemon juice
3/4 cup almonds, finely ground
1/3 cup melted butter, cooled but still liquid
toasted, sliced almonds for garnish.

Combine flour and 3 1/2 tablespoons of sugar, mixing well. Add softened butter and combine until crumbly. Beat 1 egg and mix well into the pastry. Form into a ball. Chill pastry for at least 30 minutes. Roll out to uniform thickness for a 9-inch tart baking form. Weight down pastry shell or prick bottom of shell with a fork.

Partially cook the tart shell in a 375°F oven for 8 minutes. Meanwhile, with a whisk, beat together the remaining eggs, sugar, lemon rind, juice and almonds. Add melted butter and continue beating.

Pour the lemon mixture into the tart shell and bake at 375°F for an additional 25 to 30 minutes, until done. Remove from oven and allow the tart to cool. Garnish with toasted sliced almonds. Serves 8.

110

Rustico Bay, Prince Edward Island

COCONUT CREAM PIE
The West Point Lighthouse

This coconut cream pie recipe is for those who have difficulty making perfect meringue. Simply omit it and serve with a dollop of freshly whipped cream.

3/4 cup sugar
1/3 cup flour
2 tablespoons cornstarch
2 cups milk
2 eggs, beaten
1/2 cup sweetened coconut
baked pastry shell
1/2 cup heavy cream (35% m.f.)

In a large saucepan, combine sugar, flour and cornstarch. Gradually stir in milk. Bring mixture to a boil, stirring constantly, until it thickens. Cook over medium heat 2 minutes longer, then remove from heat. Stir small amount of hot mixture into eggs, return to hot mixture and cook two minutes, stirring constantly. Remove from heat and stir in coconut. Pour into a cooked prepared pie shell. Cool and top with whipped cream before serving. Serves 6 to 8.

PRIZE BUTTER TARTS
The West Point Lighthouse

These tasty little tarts store well and are delicious with a freshly brewed pot of tea.

1 cup brown sugar
1/3 cup butter, melted
1 teaspoon vanilla
1 egg, beaten
2 tablespoons milk
10 to 12 unbaked pastry tart shells

Mix together sugar, butter and vanilla. Stir in the egg and milk. Pour into prepared tart shells and bake 400°F for 15 minutes.

Picking strawberries

STRAWBERRIES IN PUFF PASTRY
The Loyalist Country Inn

What an impressive dessert to serve your favourite Valentine — or have your Valentine serve you!

6 to 8 puff pastry hearts or rounds (3 to 4
    inches each)
1 quart fresh strawberries, sliced. Reserve 12
    berries for garnish.
1 recipe Grand Marnier Pastry Cream

Prepare puff pastries from a 14-ounce package of frozen puff pastry, following package directions. Cool on a wire rack and split.

    Wash and slice berries, adding a small amount of sugar, if desired.

Pastry Cream
1 cup milk
2 egg yolks
1/4 cup sugar
2 tablespoons flour
1 1/2 tablespoons Grand Marnier
1 cup heavy cream, whipped
1 teaspoon icing sugar

Heat milk almost to boiling. In a bowl, beat egg yolks well with sugar; beat in flour. Slowly mix half the hot milk into the egg mixture, then gradually stir back into the remaining milk. Cook over low heat until the custard thickens and barely starts to boil. Remove from heat and cool over ice, stirring often. When completely cool stir in Grand Marnier. Whip cream and fold into milk-egg mixture. (Reserve a small amount of cream to use as a garnish).

    Split hearts and spoon pastry cream onto bottom halves. Place sliced berries on the cream. Place top half of hearts over berries and sprinkle remaining berries around hearts on plates. Dust pastries with icing sugar and garnish with whipped cream and fanned whole strawberries. Serves 6 to 8.

DOUBLE CHOCOLATE MARBLE CHEESECAKE
The Loyalist Country Inn

If you think all cheesecakes were created equal, try this treat from PEI's Loyalist Country Inn.

2 2/3 cups chocolate cookie crumbs
2/3 cup butter, melted
1 pound cream cheese, softened
1/2 cup sugar
1 cup heavy cream (35% m.f.)
1 1/2 package unflavoured gelatin softened in
    1/4 cup cold water
1/4 cup boiling water
1 ounce white crème de cacao
1 ounce brown crème de cacao
4 ounces white chocolate, melted and cooled
4 ounces milk chocolate, melted and cooled
1 cup heavy cream, whipped
Chocolate curls, or fresh berries and whipped
    cream for garnish

Combine chocolate cookie crumbs and melted butter and press into bottom and sides of 10-inch springform pan. Bake at 350°F for 10 minutes. Cool completely.

Beat cream cheese with sugar until light and fluffy. Add 1 cup of cream and continue beating.

Dissolve softened gelatin in 1/4 cup boiling water. Add gelatin to cheese mixture. Divide mixture in half. Add white crème de cacao and white chocolate to one half of mixture. Add brown crème de cacao and milk chocolate to remaining mixture. Divide whipped cream and fold half into each of the cheese mixtures. Swirl the two mixtures together over chocolate crumb crust, in springform pan. Chill 4 hours or overnight until set.

Garnish with whipped cream, chocolate curls, fresh berries or **raspberry coulis**. Serves 12 to 16.

Raspberry Coulis
6 cups fresh or frozen unsweetened raspberries
2/3 cup sugar or to taste
3 tablespoons cornstarch
1/4 cup water

Heat raspberries and sugar to boiling, strain well to discard seeds. Thicken with cornstarch mixed with water. Cool. Serve either under cheesecake on a plate or drizzle over top.

Bright House

RHUBARB CRISP
The Bright House

This rendition of an old fashioned fruit crisp is easy to prepare and a wonderful winter dessert. At the Bright House it is served with whipped cream!

3-4 cups rhubarb, chopped small
1/2 cup orange juice
3/4 cup sugar
1/2 teaspoon cinnamon
1 tablespoon butter
3/4 cup flour
3/4 cup brown sugar
3/4 cup rolled oats
3/4 cup flaked coconut
1/2 cup butter or margarine

Preheat oven to 350°F and grease a 9 x 9-inch baking dish. Combine rhubarb, orange juice and cinnamon and place in prepared pan. Dot with butter.

For the topping combine flour, sugar, rolled oats, coconut and butter with a pastry blender. Sprinkle over rhubarb. Bake until golden brown and bubbly, approximately 45 minutes.

Digby Neck

INDIVIDUAL CHEESECAKES WITH STRAWBERRY SAUCE
The Mountain Gap Inn

We tested these little cheesecakes at the height of the berry season. If you use frozen berries, we suggest you make a cooked sauce.

16 ounces cream cheese
1/3 teaspoon vanilla
2/3 cup sugar
4 teaspoons flour
dash of salt
zest and juice of 1 lemon
2 eggs
3 tablespoons blend
1 quart fresh strawberries, washed and hulled
1 tablespoon lemon juice
1/4 cup sugar, or to taste
1/2 cup heavy cream, whipped

Place cream cheese in a large mixing bowl and beat to soften. Add vanilla and sugar and beat until fluffy. Blend in flour and salt. Add lemon zest and juice and beat in eggs, one at a time. Beat in blend.

Grease 6 to 8 custard cups and line with plastic wrap. Fill three-quarters full with cheese mixture and place in a pan with 1/4-inch of water at the bottom. Bake at 350°F, until just set, about 20 minutes. Remove from oven and cool. Chill at least 2 hours before removing from cups.

For the sauce, prepare berries and slice into a bowl. Reserve 6 to 8 small berries for a garnish. Squeeze lemon juice over top and add sugar. Stir to coat and refrigerate a few hours, stirring occasionally.

To serve, unmold cheesecake onto serving plate. Spoon sauce over and garnish with whipped cream and small berries, if desired.

GERMAN RASPBERRY POUNDCAKE
The Braeside Inn

The Braeside serves this dessert warm with ice cream, whipped cream, fresh raspberries or raspberry sauce, but it may also be served cold.

1 cup butter
1 1/4 cup sugar
4 eggs, lightly beaten

1 3/4 cups flour
1 pint fresh raspberries

In a mixer, blend butter and sugar until creamy, about 3 minutes. Add egg and flour in three additions and whip at high speed for 7 minutes. Grease a 9-inch springform pan. Line the bottom with waxed paper and flour the sides. Spread half of the batter in the pan. Add the berries to form a uniform layer and spoon remaining batter over raspberries.

Bake in a preheated 350°F oven for approximately 1 hour or until cake leaves sides of pan and springs back when lightly touched in center.

VINEYARD'S CARROT TORTE
Chez La Vigne

This torte improves with age: prepare it a couple of days before you intend to serve it.

5 egg yolks
1 1/2 cups sugar
lemon zest of 2 lemons
juice of 1 lemon
1/2 pound almonds, ground
1/2 pound carrots, finely grated
1/2 cup cornstarch
1/4 teaspoon cinnamon
1/4 teaspoon cloves
1 tablespoon baking powder
pinch of salt
5 egg whites, beaten to a stiff peak
3 1/2 tablespoons Kirsch
1/4 cup apricot jelly or puréed jam

Beat egg yolks, sugar, lemon juice and zest until thick and pale. Fold in almonds and grated carrots. Combine cornstarch, cinnamon, cloves, baking powder and salt. Mix lightly, but well, into batter. Fold egg whites and Kirsch into batter.

Line the bottom of a high, round 10-inch cake pan with oiled paper. Pour the batter into the pan and cook in a preheated 350°F oven for 1 hour or until centre springs back when lightly touched. Remove from the oven and while still hot, brush with apricot jelly. Glaze the torte with light royal icing or decorate with small marzipan carrots.

Captain Burgess Rum Cake (Blomidon Inn)

CAPTAIN BURGESS RUM CAKE
Blomidon Inn

This is probably the Blomidon Inn's best known dessert. Store your version for a day or two to let the rum flavour mellow.

3/4 cup softened butter
1 1/2 cups granulated sugar
4 large eggs
3 cups all purpose flour
1/4 teaspoon salt
4 1/2 teaspoons baking powder
1/2 cup dark rum
1 cup milk
1 cup raisins
1 cup chopped pecans
1/4 cup pecan halves
1/4 cup butter, melted
1/4 cup water
1 cup granulated sugar
1/4 cup dark rum

Grease a 10-inch tube pan and line with waxed paper.

Cream together butter and sugar until fluffy. Add eggs, one at a time, beating after each addition.

In a separate bowl, combine flour, salt and baking powder. Add dry ingredients to creamed mixture, alternately with rum and milk, being careful to mix only until batter is smooth. Fold in the raisins and chopped pecans.

Place halved pecans on the bottom of the tube pan. Spread the cake batter evenly over the nuts and bake at 350°F for 55 to 60 minutes, or until a toothpick inserted in center of the cake comes out clean. Turn the cake onto a rack to cool, before glazing.

In a small saucepan combine butter, water, sugar and rum and place over medium heat until sugar is dissolved. Prick the cake with a small skewer and drizzle the syrup over the cake until it is all absorbed. Store in a tightly sealed container at a cool temperature to mellow before serving. Yields 12 to 14 servings.

Avondale near Windsor, N.S.

HOT APPLE CAKE WITH CARAMEL PECAN SAUCE
St. Martins Country Inn

Desserts that have fruit or vegetables as ingredients, such as zucchini, carrot and apple cakes have a delicious flavour that improves if left for a day or two. This recipe with its accompanying pecan sauce will not likely survive that long.

1 cup unsalted butter, softened
1 cup sugar
2 eggs
1 teaspoon vanilla
1 1/2 cups all purpose flour
1 1/2 teaspoons cinnamon
1 teaspoon baking soda
1/4 teaspoon salt
4 medium tart apples, peeled, cored and finely
   chopped
3/4 cup pecans, coarsely chopped

In a mixer, cream butter and sugar until fluffy, approximately 3 minutes. On low speed, beat in eggs, one at a time and add vanilla.

Sift together dry ingredients and add to the batter, stirring just until mixed. Blend in apples and pecans.

Spoon batter into a greased 7 x 11-inch oblong cake pan and bake in a preheated 350°F oven for 35 to 45 minutes, until top is golden and a toothpick inserted in center of cake comes out clean. Cool in pan for 10 minutes before turning out on a rack.

Serve cake warm with vanilla ice-cream on the side and topped with **Caramel Pecan Sauce**.

Caramel Pecan Sauce
2 tablespoons unsalted butter
1/4 cup pecan halves
1/2 cup dark, brown sugar, packed
1/2 cup heavy cream (35% m.f.)
1 tablespoon bourbon or rum

In a small saucepan, over moderately-high heat, melt butter. Add nuts and cook, stirring constantly, until nuts are toasted and butter is light brown. Add sugar and cream. Continue to stir as sugar dissolves and the sauce boils, turning a deep golden brown. Remove from heat, add rum and cool.

Near Middleton in the Annapolis Valley

BLUEBERRY CAKE
Cobequid Inn

This is a cake that the whole family will enjoy. Served warm, cold or straight from the pan it will be gone before you know it.

1 cup butter
1 cup sugar
2 eggs
1/2 teaspoon lemon extract
2 cups all purpose flour
2 teaspoons baking powder
3/4 cup milk
1 cup blueberries, fresh or frozen
1/4 teaspoon cinnamon
3/4 cup brown sugar

Cream butter and sugar until light and fluffy. Beat in eggs and lemon extract. Sift flour and baking powder and add to batter alternately with milk, in two additions. Stir in blueberries and pour batter in 8 x 8-inch cake pan which has been lined with waxed paper. Combine cinnamon and brown sugar and sprinkle over batter.

Bake in a preheated 350°F oven for 35 to 45 minutes, until a toothpick inserted in the center of the cake comes out clean. Note, the cake takes the longer cooking time if using frozen berries.

RHUBARB COCONUT SQUARES
The Mountain Gap Inn

Chef Hank Lewis at Mountain Gap suggests that for these squares you leave the rhubarb filling rather tart because the topping is quite sweet.

Base
1 1/3 cups all purpose flour
1/2 cup unsalted butter
1/2 cup sugar
zest of 1/2 an orange

Filling
2 cups rhubarb, washed and diced
sugar to taste
juice of one orange
2 tablespoons butter
dash of freshly grated nutmeg

Topping
2 eggs
3/4 cup sugar (second amount)
2 1/2 cups long shredded coconut
1 1/2 teaspoon vanilla
2 tablespoons flour
zest of half an orange

Blend together the first 4 ingredients until mealy. Spread evenly in a greased 9 x 9-inch pan and press down firmly.

Boil together rhubarb, sugar and orange juice until the mixture thickens. Remove from the heat and stir in butter and nutmeg. Allow to cool slightly and then spread over crust.

For the topping, blend together eggs, sugar, coconut, vanilla, flour and zest. Spread over filling and bake squares at 350°F until lightly browned, about 25 to 30 minutes. Allow to cool before cutting into squares.

MAPLE MOUSSE
Loon Bay Lodge

The chef at Loon Bay Lodge admits that all this cream is bad for the heart, but tells us, "It is oh so good for the soul."

3 eggs, separated
3/4 cup pure maple syrup
1/3 teaspoon vanilla
1 cup heavy cream (35% m.f.)
Whipped cream and toasted slivered almonds
    for garnish

Beat egg yolks and blend in maple syrup. Place mixture in a heavy saucepan and cook over low heat, stirring constantly, until it reaches the consistency of soft custard, about 10 minutes. Remove from heat, add vanilla and cool.

Whip cream and fold into cooled custard. Beat egg whites until stiff and fold into custard. Pour into parfait glasses and freeze until firm.

Let stand at room temperature for 10 to 15 minutes before serving. Garnish with whipped cream and toasted almond slivers, if desired. Serves 6.

CRANACHAN
Glenora Inn and Distillery

This traditional Scottish dessert, known also as "Fardach", was served locally on Hallowe'en. A wedding ring or button was stirred into the dessert. Family and friends would each take a spoon and eat from the same bowl. The lucky one to retrieve the ring would be the next to marry.

3/4 cup oatmeal, toasted
1 1/2 cups heavy cream (35% m.f.)
1/3 cup icing sugar, sifted
3/4 teaspoon vanilla
fresh blueberries
2 ounces dark rum

Place oatmeal on a baking sheet and cook in a preheated 350°F oven until golden, about 6 to 8 minutes; cool and reserve. Whip cream with sugar and vanilla until firm. Stir in cooled oatmeal. Spoon mixture into four serving dishes and top with fresh blueberries (or fresh fruit of choice). Garnish with fresh mint or a lime twist and drizzle 1/2 ounce of rum over top. The Glenora Inn uses Smuggler's Cove, their own brand of rum. Serves 4.

MAPLE SUGAR CRÈME BRULÉE
Dalvay-by-the-Sea

For a lighter crème brulée you may substitute milk or blend (12% m.f.) or any combination of milk, blend and cream for the heavy cream in this recipe. Dalvay-by-the-Sea accompanies this dessert with sugared almond cookies.

1/2 cup maple syrup
2 cups heavy cream (35% m.f.)
1/2 vanilla bean, split or 1/2 teaspoon vanilla
    extract
zest of 1/2 lemon, cut fine
1/2 cinnamon stick, crushed
6 egg yolks
1 1/2 teaspoon sugar

Bring maple syrup to a boil. Simmer for 2 minutes, remove from heat and let cool. In a saucepan, slowly bring cream, vanilla, lemon zest and cinnamon to a boil. Meanwhile, beat yolks and sugar until thick and pale in colour. Whisk boiling cream mixture into yolks. Return mixture to saucepan and stir over low heat until thick.

Strain cream into a cold bowl which is set in ice and whisk rapidly. Fold maple syrup into the chilled custard. Fill small chilled *pots de crème*, or custard cups, to rim and refrigerate overnight. Before serving, sprinkle white sugar and spray a light coat of water on top of creams. Place custards under a preheated broiler to brown. Serve immediately. Serves 4.

Garrison House

STRAWBERRIES WITH CITRUS RIESLING SABAYON
The Garrison House Inn

There is nothing to compare to the sweet juicy taste of your first strawberry of the season. Unless of course you choose to try this superb recipe from Patrick Redgrave's kitchen. The winner will be hard to choose.

3 egg yolks
3 tablespoons sugar
2 teaspoons mixed orange/lemon zest (thinly cut peel)
1/2 cup Riesling wine
1/3 cup heavy cream (35% m.f.)
2 teaspoons Cointreau (or other orange liqueur)
1 quart fresh strawberries, hulled
2 tablespoons dark bitter chocolate, grated
sprigs of mint leaves

Beat egg yolks, sugar and citrus zest until thick, about 5 minutes. Put yolk mixture in top of a double boiler over simmering water, and gradually whisk in the wine. Continue whisking until the mixture will stick to the back of a spoon, approximately 7 minutes. Remove from heat and cool mixture over a bowl of ice water.

Whip cream and liqueur and fold into chilled sabayon. Arrange berries in dessert dishes and spoon sabayon over them. Dust with grated chocolate and garnish with fresh mint. Serves 4.

BREAD AND BUTTER PUDDING WITH STRAWBERRY SAUCE
La Poissonnière

Remember the bread puddings from your grandmother's kitchen? Richard Chiasson's modern version will satisfy the most discriminating palate.

2 cups strawberries, cleaned and sliced
1/2 cup sugar (for sauce)
1 teaspoon cornstarch
3 teaspoons cold water
9 slices of stale bread
1/4 cup soft butter
4 eggs
3 tablespoons sugar

Annapolis Royal Gardens

1/4 teaspoon vanilla
1/4 teaspoon salt
2 1/2 cups milk, scalded
cinnamon and nutmeg for garnish

Prepare strawberries and place in a bowl. Add 1/2 cup of sugar and let sit, refrigerated, 24 hours. Drain juice from berries into a small saucepan and set over medium heat until it begins to boil. Combine cornstarch and water and add to strawberry juice. Once thickened, remove from heat and cool. Add strawberries.

Preheat oven to 350°F. Butter each slice of bread, then cut into 1/2 inch squares. Grease 6 individual ramekin dishes and divide bread cubes between them. In a mixing bowl combine eggs, sugar, vanilla and salt. Gradually stir in hot, scalded milk, then pour mixture over bread pieces. Sprinkle with nutmeg and cinnamon. Set dishes in a pan containing 1 inch of hot water. Bake 35 to 40 minutes or until set. Invert onto serving plates, and serve hot or cold with strawberry sauce. At La Poissonnière patrons are treated to whipped cream! Serves 6.

ORANGE YOGHURT MOUSSE
The Normaway Inn

This is a low-fat winner — easy to prepare, healthy and refreshing.

1 envelope unflavoured gelatin
1/4 cup warm water
4 tablespoons sugar (optional, 4 packets of
    Nutrasweet)
2 cups fresh orange juice reduced to 1/2 cup
    or 1/2 cup frozen orange juice concentrate
2 cups low-fat unflavoured yoghurt
1 1/2 cups fruit (raspberries, strawberries,
    blueberries etc.)
1 tablespoon sugar (2nd amount)
1 teaspoon fresh lemon juice
fresh mint leaves, as garnish

Sprinkle gelatin over water and let stand for 5 minutes to soften. Heat gelatin over low setting until it dissolves. Add sugar and stir to dissolve.

If using fresh orange juice, reduce over medium heat to 1/2 cup. Pour orange juice into bowl and briskly whisk in the yoghurt, being careful not to over process. Stir in gelatin mixture. Pour mousse into 4 parfait glasses or 6 ramekins and refrigerate until set.

Combine fruit, sugar (2nd amount) and lemon juice in a food processor and purée. Strain purée through a fine sieve and refrigerate.

To serve, pour fruit purée over desserts and garnish with fresh mint. Serves 4 to 6.

CRÈME CARAMEL
Strathgartney Country Inn

Prepare your crème caramels early in the day so that they are well chilled before being turned out on the serving plates.

Caramel glaze
1/2 cup sugar
1 1/2 tablespoons water

Custard
2 cups milk
3/4 cup confectioners' sugar
2 egg yolks
4 whole eggs
1 teaspoon vanilla
Fresh fruit, as garnish (optional)

Have ready 6 lightly greased custard cups.

Heat sugar for caramel glaze in a saucepan. Begin to stir when it starts to melt around the edges, then stir slowly but continuously. When it is fully melted, cautiously stir in the water all at once. Divide caramel evenly among custard cups.

Heat milk and sugar until almost boiling. In a large bowl, combine yolks and whole eggs, then gradually stir in the hot milk. Strain into custard cups. Place custard cups in pan with 1/4 inch of water. Bake at 400°F for 20 minutes.

Let the custard cool thoroughly, then run a knife around the inside of the cup before unmolding on serving plate. Garnish with fresh fruit.

Presqu'ile, N.S.

Acton's Stoneground Wholewheat Bread

8 BREADS

Breads, rolls or muffins accompany most meals in Maritime cuisine and this is a small sampling of some of our best recipes. While some directions are time consuming, we feel that all could be prepared with excellent results by a novice cook.

Acton's *Stoneground Wholewheat Bread* and *Maritime Brown Bread* from the Compass Rose on Grand Manan Island in New Brunswick are yeast breads and obviously take time to prepare. Nicholas Pierce of *Acton's Grill and Café* buys his stoneground wholewheat flour from a local farm and the *Maritime Brown Bread* includes the traditional ingredients of molasses and rolled oats.

Also included are a number of healthy and easily prepared quick breads. Golden yellow *Corn Bread* from MacAskill's Restaurant is a wonderful accompaniment to hearty winter meals while *Purple Violet Bread* from Shirley Ayles' kitchen at the Aylesford Inn includes wild violets for taste and decoration.

Acton's Stoneground Wholewheat Bread

ACTON'S STONEGROUND WHOLEWHEAT BREAD
Acton's Grill and Café

The bread at Acton's is made daily and is so popular with guests that they often ask for a second basket to be brought to the table.

2 fresh yeast cakes or 2 packages active dry
    yeast
2 cups warm water
1 tablespoon sugar
1 tablespoon salt
1 tablespoon olive oil (or vegetable oil)
2 to 2 1/2 cups all purpose flour
3 cups wholewheat flour (preferably
    stoneground)

Dissolve the yeast in the warm water along with the sugar, salt and oil. Add 1 cup of all purpose flour and whisk together well. Let this "sponge" proof for 45 minutes in a warm place.

Add remaining flours and work into a soft but not sticky dough. Depending on the quality of the flour, you may need a little more to get desired consistency. Place dough in a lightly greased bowl, turning once to grease surface. Cover and let rise, in a warm place, until double in size, about 1 hour.

Punch down dough and form into 2 free-form oval loaves. Place on greased cookie sheet, cover and let rise again, until doubled, about 45 minutes. Bake in preheated 400°F oven for 25 to 30 minutes. Bread is cooked if hollow sounding when tapped on bottom. Brush tops with melted butter if desired. Makes two large loaves.

Acton's Grill and Café

CORNMEAL BREAD
MacAskill's Restaurant

Cornmeal gives a lovely flavour and colour to breads and muffins and this recipe is no exception. The recipe makes two large loaves, one to savour while it is still warm and one to freeze for a busy day.

1 2/3 cups cornmeal
2 cups water
1 1/2 cups sugar
3/4 cup shortening
1 1/2 teaspoons salt
3 eggs
3 1/2 cups flour
1/3 cup whey powder (or skim milk powder)
2 tablespoons baking powder

Soak cornmeal in water in a bowl. In a mixer, cream sugar, shortening and salt until light and fluffy. Add eggs, one at a time. Sift together flour, whey powder and baking powder. Add to batter, mixing until dry ingredients are just incorporated. Slowly add cornmeal, scraping bowl often, until it is completely blended. Increase speed and beat for 2 minutes.

Grease and flour two 8 x 4-inch loaf pans and divide batter between them. Bake in preheated 350°F oven for 45 to 50 minutes until a toothpick inserted in center comes out clean. Makes 2 loaves.

Cornmeal Bread (MacAskill's Restaurant)

Hole-in-the-Wall at Grand Manan

MARITIME BROWN BREAD
The Compass Rose, N.B.

Truly a traditional Maritime bread, this molasses laced brown bread recipe makes two loaves and is a pleasant accompaniment to a hearty meal.

1 cup rolled oats
2 teaspoons salt
2 tablespoons lard
1/2 cup molasses
2 cups boiling water
1 package yeast
1/2 cup warm water
1 teaspoon molasses (2nd amount)
5 cups white flour

In a large bowl combine rolled oats, salt, lard, molasses and boiling water and stir until lard dissolves. Cool to lukewarm.

Stir 1 teaspoon molasses into 1/2 cup lukewarm water, sprinkle yeast over top and stir to dissolve. When yeast has doubled in size, add to rolled oats mixture. Stir in flour, a cupful at a time. Turn onto a floured board and knead until smooth, 4 to 5 minutes. Shape into a ball and place in a lightly greased bowl, turning once to grease surface. Cover and let rise in a warm place until double, about 1 hour.

Punch down dough, divide in half and shape into two loaves. Place in greased 9 x 5-inch pans. Cover and let rise about 1 hour.

Bake in a preheated 350°F oven, 30 to 40 minutes. Remove from pans and cool on wire racks. Yields 2 loaves.

DOWN DRURY LANE WHITE ROLLS
Drury Lane Steak House

These rolls are economical, easy to prepare and good enough to make this a basic recipe for your files.

2 teaspoons sugar
1/2 cup lukewarm water
1 1/2 tablespoons dry yeast (1 1/2 packages)
3 cups hot water
1/4 cup shortening
1 tablespoon salt
1 tablespoon sugar
8 to 9 cups all purpose flour

Dissolve sugar in warm water. Sprinkle yeast over top and let stand in a warm place for 10 to 15 minutes. In a large bowl, add shortening, salt and sugar to hot water. Stir and let cool while the yeast is proofing. When the hot water has cooled to 85°F, whisk in the yeast mixture. Stir in flour, 2 cups at a time, until you cannot stir any more. Let the batter rest for 10 minutes.

Turn batter onto a floured surface and knead, adding more flour as necessary to prevent sticking, until, as the chef says, "'the cows come home," approximately 10 to 12 minutes. Place dough in a greased bowl, turn to coat, cover and let rise until doubled in size, 1 to 1 1/2 hours. Punch down dough, shape into rolls and place in greased muffin tins. Cover and let rise for 30 minutes, until doubled. Bake in a preheated 350°F oven for 15 minutes or until golden brown. Remove from oven. Brush with melted butter and immediately remove from pans. Makes 3 1/2 to 4 dozen.

NOVA SCOTIA OATCAKES
The Palliser

It is said that Scottish settlers brought their recipe for oatcakes to Canada's shores. The twentieth-century version continues to be popular with everyone, regardless of its country of origin.

1 1/2 cups flour
1/4 teaspoon soda
1/4 teaspoon baking powder
generous dash of salt
1 1/2 cups oatmeal
1/2 cup brown sugar
1/2 cup shortening
1/2 cup butter or margarine
2 1/2 tablespoons water
1/4 teaspoon vanilla

Mix the dry ingredients in a large bowl. Cut in shortening and butter with pastry blender. Add water and vanilla. Roll out on a floured surface to 1/4-inch thickness. Cut in squares and place on a greased cookie sheet. Bake at 375°F for 10 to 12 minutes, until golden brown. Yields 12 to 16 oatcakes.

NUT AND SEEDS BREAD
Bluenose Lodge

This loaf keeps very well, wrapped and refrigerated. It is delicious served with Liptauer cheese.

2 1/4 cups white flour
3/4 cup whole wheat flour
1 1/2 teaspoons baking powder
1 1/2 teaspoons baking soda
3/4 teaspoon salt
1 1/2 cups brown sugar, lightly packed
1/2 cup chopped nuts (walnuts, pecans etc.)
3 tablespoons wheat germ
3 tablespoons sesame seeds
3 tablespoons poppy seeds
2 eggs
1/3 cup + 1 tablespoon vegetable oil
1 1/2 cups buttermilk

In a large bowl combine all dry ingredients and mix thoroughly. In a separate bowl beat together eggs, oil and buttermilk. Add liquid to dry ingredients and stir until just mixed. Pour batter into a greased and floured 9 x 5-inch loaf pan. Bake in a preheated 350°F oven for 55 to 60 minutes or until a tester inserted in center of loaf, comes out clean. Cool a few minutes and then turn out on wire rack.

PURPLE VIOLET BREAD
Aylesford Inn

The purple violet is the floral emblem of New Brunswick, adopted in 1936 at the request of the Women's Institute. How fitting for Shirley Ayles to incorporate this beautiful and edible flower into her tea bread.

3 cups all purpose flour
1 cup white sugar
1 tablespoon baking powder
1/2 teaspoon salt
1/4 teaspoon baking soda
1 egg
1 2/3 cups milk
1/4 cup vegetable oil
1/2 cup walnuts, chopped
3 tablespoons violet flowers
2 tablespoons brown sugar

In a large bowl, stir together flour, white sugar, baking powder, salt and baking soda. Beat together egg, milk and oil and add to the flour mixture, stirring just until combined. Set aside 10 of the violets. Gently stir the walnuts and remaining violets into the batter.

Divide batter into two greased 7 1/2 x 3 1/2-inch loaf pans. Gently press reserved violets into the batter in each pan and sprinkle tops with brown sugar. Bake in a preheated 350°F oven for 40 to 45 minutes, until a toothpick inserted in centre of bread comes out clean. Cool in pans for 10 minutes, remove and cool on wire racks.

May be served warm or cool. Makes 2 loaves.

Bluenose Lodge

BERRY LAYER MUFFINS
Auberge Le Heron Country Inn

You can use whatever fruit is in season to give these wonderful little muffins a change of flavour. Make a double batch and freeze half to enjoy later.

1/3 cup butter
2/3 cup brown sugar
2 eggs
3/4 cup milk
1/2 teaspoon vanilla
2 cups flour
4 teaspoons baking powder
1/2 teaspoon salt
3/4 cup fresh whole berries (for example,
    blueberries, raspberries)
2 tablespoons sugar
1 teaspoon cinnamon

Cream together butter and brown sugar until fluffy. Beat in eggs, milk and vanilla; don't be alarmed if mixture curdles.

Sift together flour, baking powder and salt and add, all at once to creamed mixture stirring just enough to dampen dry ingredients.

Grease 12 large muffin tins and fill halfway with batter. Place a heaping spoonful of berries in centre of batter and fill tins with remaining batter. Combine sugar and cinnamon and sprinkle over muffins. Bake in preheated 375°F oven for 20 to 25 minutes. Makes 1 dozen large muffins.

CRANBERRY ORANGE MUFFINS
The Mountain Gap Inn

The chef at Mountain Gap Inn generously shared her recipe for these tart little muffins. Double your batch because they freeze well!

1 cup cranberries, coarsely chopped
1 egg, beaten
2/3 cup milk
1/3 cup butter, melted
3 tablespoons orange juice concentrate
1/2 teaspoon vanilla
zest of 1 orange
1 3/4 cups all purpose flour
2 1/2 teaspoons baking powder
1/3 cup sugar
1 teaspoon salt

Mix together cranberries, egg, milk, butter, orange juice, vanilla and zest. In a bowl, sift together the flour and baking powder and stir in the sugar and salt. Add the milk mixture to the dry ingredients, stirring just enough to blend. Spoon into paper lined muffin tins and bake at 400°F until golden, 20 to 25 minutes. Yields 12 muffins.

9 NEW BRUNSWICK

To discover the best of New Brunswick, be prepared to leave the main highways in favour of scenic backcountry roads. The largest of Canada's three Maritime Provinces, New Brunswick aptly lives up to its reputation as the "picture province." We have featured inns and restaurants in cities, nestled amid forests and along the ocean and river shores of this photographer's paradise. Scenic highlights include the Hopewell Rocks on the Fundy shore, the Kingsbrae Garden in St. Andrews, Kings Landing Historical Settlement near Fredericton and the Village Historique Acadien, a replica of an Acadian village (1770 – 1939) at Caraquet.

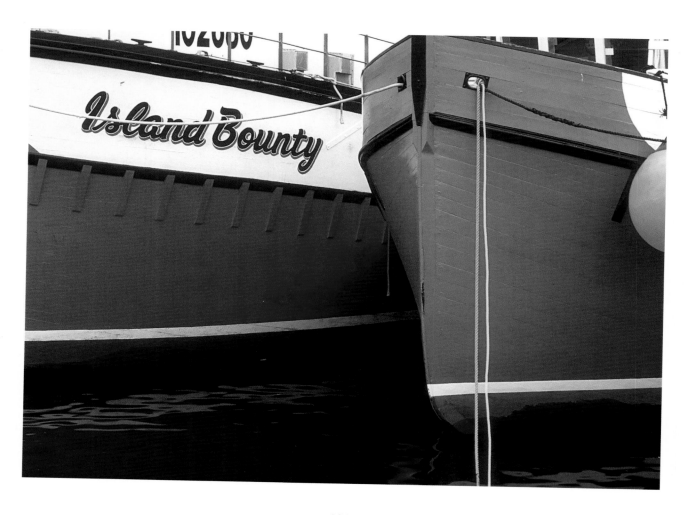

Waterford, near Sussex, N.B.

AUBERGE GABRIÈLE INN ⑩

A meal at the brightly painted Auberge Gabrièle Inn is a highlight of any visit to Shediac, the beach playground of south eastern New Brunswick. Built in 1840, this former church overlooks the glistening waters of Shediac Bay and offers travellers gracious accommodations in 15 guest rooms and suites.

The inn offers bar and table service at both lunch and dinner in a small dining room and on a large sheltered deck. Lobster "by the pound" is typical of the excellent menu that reflects the fresh seafood and produce of the region. All desserts are made on the premises.

Inn open year round; breakfast for guests only. Dining room open for lunch and dinner daily, mid-June to mid-September
Innkeeper: Pierre Landry
296 Main Street
Shediac, NB
Tel: (506) 532-8007, 1-877-982-7222
www.aubergegabriele.nb.ca

AUBERGE LES JARDINS INN ⓼

Auberge Les Jardins Inn is nestled in picturesque Saint-Jacques, on the Madawaska River just minutes from the Quebec-New Brunswick border and a mere 10 km from the city of Edmundston. The area offers visitors a variety of natural and recreational attractions including the beautiful New Brunswick Botanical Gardens and the 134-km inter-provincial Petit-Temis Hiking and Cycling Trail between Edmundston and Rivière-du-Loup, Quebec.

The inn features 17 luxury guestrooms decorated with a Canadiana flora motif. Accommodation is also offered in rustic housekeeping cottages as well as a 13-unit motel complex.

Specializing in creative French cuisine, the dining room is open to guests and the general

public for breakfast and dinner. The menu changes seasonally and features fresh local ingredients prepared to the highest standards.

Open year round
Innkeepers: Valmont Martin and Francine Landry
60 rue Principale

Saint-Jacques, NB
Tel: (506) 739-5514, 1-800-630-8011
www.auberge-lesjardins-inn.com

BILLY'S SEAFOOD COMPANY ⓴

Lovers of fresh seafood need look no further than Billy's Seafood Company, with its grill, fish market and oyster bar. Located in the historic City Market in the heart of uptown Saint John, Billy's sells a wide variety of local and imported fish and seafood in the market adjacent to the oyster bar.

Restaurant specials range from creamy chowder to planked salmon or a lobster chosen from the market's tank. The servers are eager to answer inquiries, and seafood purchases may be packed for travel.

Market open Monday to Saturday, 8:00 am to 6:00 pm. Restaurant open Monday to Saturday, 11:00 am to 10:00 pm, Sunday 4:00 pm to 9:00 pm
49-51 Charlotte Street
Saint John, NB
Tel: (506) 672-3474, 1-888-933-3474
www.billysseafood.com

THE BLUE DOOR RESTAURANT AND BAR ⓹

Owners Chris and Debbie Black saw the need for a modern, upbeat dining option in the capital city of Fredericton, so they opened the Blue Door. They offer a culturally varied menu specializing in freshly prepared foods — all at a reasonable price.

Start your lunch or dinner with a bowl of "yesterday's soup." Entree selections include satay, pasta, chicken, ribs and seafood. Delicious desserts include the legendary double chocolate brownies.

Open daily, year round, 11:30 am to 11:00 pm
Restaurateurs: Chris and Debbie Black
100 Regent Street
Fredericton, NB
Tel: (506) 455-2583
www.thebluedoor.ca

BOGART'S BAR AND GRILL 16

Bogart's is an elegantly appointed eatery in the centre of downtown Moncton. The long, narrow restaurant features an open kitchen design, an outdoor patio for fine weather dining and an intimate bar.

Bogart's offers extensive lunch and dinner menus. Midday, there is a wide selection of soups, chowders, salads, crêpes and wraps. Dinner choices, including fresh seafood, meats, poultry and pasta, are accompanied by suggested wine pairings. Wines are served by the glass.

Open daily, year round for lunch and dinner
Restaurateur: Brian Ritchie
589 Main Street
Moncton, NB
Tel: (506) 855-5335

CARIBBEAN FLAVA'S CASUAL 6
FINE DINING

You are in for a treat when you visit Caribbean Flava's in the heart of downtown Fredericton. Naz Ali and family hail from Trinidad and share the tastes and sounds of their former island home. The ambiance and music is warm and friendly, and the menu reflects the best of Caribbean cuisine with an emphasis on healthy dining.

In addition to the restaurant, Caribbean

Flava's offers summer dinner cruises along the scenic Saint John River: the Carleton 2 sails nightly, July and August, from Carleton Pier in downtown Fredericton. Check the restaurant or pier for details.

Open Monday through Saturday for lunch and dinner
Restaurateurs: Naz Ali and family
123 York Street
Fredericton, NB
Tel: (506) 459-1230
www.caribbeanflavas.ca

THE FAIRMONT ALGONQUIN 1

Located on a hill overlooking the historic town of St. Andrews, this full-service resort is a massive, turreted structure featuring more than 250 guestrooms. Guests enjoy tennis, swimming, cycling and golf, as well as four on-site restaurants offering superb cuisine.

St. Andrews was founded in 1783 by United Empire Loyalists. Its first residents dismantled their homes in Maine and reassembled them across Passamaquoddy Bay in New Brunswick. Nearly half the town's buildings are more than 100 years old, making a walking tour of the streets a pleasant way to spend a morning. From nearby St. George, a car ferry operates seasonally to Deer Island where another ferry will transport you to Campobello Island,

summer home of the late President Franklin Delano Roosevelt and the site of Roosevelt International Park.

Open year round
184 Adolphus Street
St. Andrews, NB
Tel: (506) 529-8823, 1-800-441-1414
www.fairmont.com

HOTEL PAULIN ⑨

Hotel Paulin was built in 1891 and purchased shortly thereafter by the current owner's grandfather. For three generations the Paulins have been providing fine food and accommodation on the Acadian shore of the Gulf of St. Lawrence.

The dining room, open to guests and the general public, features gourmet dining and, on occasion, traditional Acadian dishes. The chef prides herself on using fresh local ingredients to create seasonal menus.

Open year round. Dinner daily (reservations required by noon)
Innkeepers: Gerard R. Paulin and Karen Mersereau
143 Boulevard St-Pierre West
Caraquet, NB
Tel: (506) 727-9981
www.hotelpaulin.com

INN AT WHALE COVE ④
COTTAGES

A visit to this little gem of an inn is a step back in time. The inn is located at North Head, Grand Manan Island, a one-and-a-half hour

ferry ride from Blacks Harbour on the mainland. The main house, built in 1816, has been renovated to combine the rustic charm of hand-hewn beams with modern comforts. Antique Shaker furnishings grace three ensuite rooms. Additional accommodation is available in six cottages. Guests are invited to use the extensive library or to simply enjoy the view of Whale Cove while settling before a cozy fire in the inn's main living room.

Breakfast is included with accommodation, and lunch is served takeout-style to guests and the general public. Gourmet dinners are served daily to guests and the public, with reservations strongly suggested.

Open May through October
Innkeeper: Laura Buckley
26 Whale Cove Cottage Road
Grand Manan, NB
Tel: (506) 662-3181
www.holidayjunction.com/whalecove/

INN ON FREDERICK ②

Known to locals as the "O'Neill House," this 1840s structure has been lovingly restored to provide tranquil accommodation in seven rooms in the heart of downtown St. Andrews. The inn's location, just one block from the ocean, is perfect for exploring the area on foot. Many specialty shops, boutiques and galleries are nearby.

The European-trained chef offers fine dining each evening in the Rose Garden Dining Room to guests and the general public. Breakfast is included in the room rate; Sunday brunch is open to all.

Open year round. Dinner daily, Sunday brunch
Innkeepers: Jim and Joyce Crouch
58 Frederick Street
St. Andrews-by-the-Sea, NB
Tel: (506) 529-2603, 1-877-895-4400
www.innonfrederick.ca

INN ON THE COVE & SPA 22

This small inn and day spa, perched on the banks of the Bay of Fundy, offers a serene pastoral setting only five minutes from the centre of the busy port city of Saint John. You can enjoy the cozy fire-lit rooms and revel in the radiance of moonlight dancing across the water along with the flash of Partridge Island lighthouse.

The innkeepers have had a distinguished career in food preparation and writing. They were hosts to more than 100 episodes of *Tides Table*, a Maritime TV cooking show, and are the authors of two cookbooks as well as many newspaper and

magazine articles. Breakfast is served to inn guests only, and a spa lunch is available exclusively to those attending the day spa.

Open year round. Gourmet oceanside suppers Monday to Saturday for guests and the general public
Innkeepers: Ross and Willa Mavis
1371 Sand Cove Road
Saint John, NB
Tel: (506) 672-7799
www.innonthecove.com

LE FLAIR RESTAURANT AT 14 WILD ROSE INN

This elegant inn, a short drive from Moncton in a rolling countryside setting, offers 16 guestrooms and suites. Guests are invited to relax fireside, enjoy an activity in the games room or play a round at the adjacent golf course. The inn is a favourite for weekend getaways and corporate events.

A gourmet breakfast is included for overnight guests and the dining room serves fresh local fare to guests and the general public.

Open year round. Lunch upon request, dinner daily
Innkeepers: Joanne and Ron Gaudet
17 Baseline Road
Lakeville, NB
Tel: (506) 383-9751, 1-888-389-7673
www.wildroseinn.com

THE LEDGES INN 7

Midway between Fredericton and the city of Miramichi, on the famed Miramichi River at Doaktown, the Ledges Inn is an inviting all-season retreat. This newly-erected log structure offers accommodation in five suites and six guest rooms.

Outdoor enthusiasts will revel in winter activities such as snowshoeing, cross-country skiing, ice fishing and riding in horse-drawn sleighs; spring and summer visitors can enjoy fly fishing on the inn's private salmon pools, bird watching and paddling; and autumn visitors will be enchanted with the colourful extravaganza of fall foliage.

Dinner is served to guests and the general public with 48-hour advance reservation.

Open year round
Innkeepers: Caroline and Everett Taylor
30 Ledges Inn Lane
Doaktown, NB
Tel: (506) 365-1820
www.ledgesinn.com

LITTLE LOUIS' OYSTER BAR 18

Well known Atlantic Canadian executive chef Stephen Huston oversees the dining room at Little Louis' Oyster Bar and offers patrons a unique dining and entertainment experience. Though located away from Moncton's downtown hub, the restaurant and bar are well worth visiting.

Oysters are a specialty at the restaurant — naturally — but diners will also find a varied selection of carefully prepared and executed appetizers, entrées and desserts.

Open year round. Lunch Tuesday to Friday, dinner daily, live jazz entertainment Thursday to Saturday at 5:00 pm
Restaurateurs: Deborah and Dana Snitch
245 Collishaw Street, 2nd floor
Moncton, NB
Tel: (506) 855-2022
www.littlelouis.ca

LITTLE SHEMOGUE COUNTRY INN 12

Tucked away on the shores of Northumberland Strait, Little Shemogue Country Inn offers a serene retreat. Innkeeper Petra Sudbrack's talents as an interior designer are very evident in the inn. The house, which offers five guest rooms and several small, intimate dining rooms, is filled with early Canadian and European antiques. Ideally suited for longer stays, an annex offers four suites plus a common room for meetings or private receptions.

Whether it is breakfast or dinner, gourmet surprises such as the inn's own smoked salmon,

are always in store. A five-course candlelight dinner is served at a 7:00 pm sitting to guests and the general public, with advance reservations.

Open year round
Innkeepers: Petra and Klaus Sudbrack
Little Shemogue, NB
Tel: (506) 538-2320
www.little-inn.nb.ca

MARSHLANDS INN 13

A stately pre-confederation inn and coach house, Marshlands Inn offers accommodation in 18 antique-furnished guest rooms in the university town of Sackville. Surrounded by lush gardens, this tranquil establishment features inviting nooks, dormer windows and fireside seats ideal for reading and relaxation.

The inn takes its name from the Tantramar Marshes that surround the town. This area lies along one of the main North American migratory bird routes and provides opportunities to view many species of waterfowl and other birds as they come to rest on the marshy flats each spring and fall.

The dining room at Marshlands offers a wide choice of dishes, including home-prepared pâtés, creamy chowders, hearty steaks and fresh Atlantic salmon.

Open year round
Innkeepers: Lucy and Barry Dane
55 Bridges Street
Sackville, NB
Tel: (506) 536-0170, 1-800-561-1266
www.marshlands.nb.ca

OPERA BISTRO

Noted chef Alex Begner brings his talents to Opera Bistro, a new eatery in Saint John's uptown district. This neat little bistro, with a courtyard area for sunny weather, serves smaller-

sized portions or tapas plus regular entrées for evening dining.

As an added convenience, the Begners operate Operaieto (Little Opera) around the corner at 2 King Street, where lunch or dinner items are available takeout style.

Open Monday to Saturday, 8:00 am to 11:00 pm and Sunday 3:00 pm to 10:00 pm
60 Prince William Street
Saint John, NB
Restaurateur/Chef: Alex Begner
Tel: (506) 642-2822
www.operabistro.com

PASTALLI ITALIAN CUCINA 17

Pastalli, located in the heart of downtown Moncton, is decorated with a stylish Mediterranean flavour. The semi-open design features mellow golden and brown hues accented with artwork and the innovative use of wood. Diners may choose to enjoy their meal in a small main dining room, in an alcove overlooking the open kitchen or, in season, on the terrace.

The cuisine is Mediterranean with international accents. Guests are invited to start their meal with a trip to the bread bar where they grill their own bread with a variety of seasoned butters. This is followed by a choice of salads, appetizers, pasta, specialty wood-fired pizzas, meat and seafood entrées and desserts.

Open daily, year round for lunch and dinner
Restaurateur: Gilles Ratte
611 Main Street

Moncton, NB
Tel: (506) 383-1050
www.lunchonline.ca

ROSSMOUNT INN

At Rossmount Inn you step back in time to the genteel, romantic Victorian era. The property is part of a private 35-hectare estate at the foot of Chamcook Mountain, overlooking Passamaquoddy Bay. The inn encompasses a three-storey manor house with 18 guest rooms and a cottage available for weekly or monthly rental. Located minutes from the picturesque town of St. Andrews and the Atlantic Salmon Interpretive Centre, the property offers scenic hiking and nature trails with spectacular panoramic views.

Fresh local ingredients, highlighted by produce from the inn's kitchen garden, have won the restaurant a well-deserved reputation for exceptional European-style fine dining. Expect the menu to change daily to offer the best in-season ingredients.

Open March 30 through December
Innkeepers: Chris and Graziella Aerni
4599 Route 127
St. Andrews by-the-Sea
New Brunswick, NB
Tel: (506) 529-3351
www.rossmountinn.com

SEBASTIAN

Sebastian serves great food in an urban ambiance. Located in a refurbished Victorian building in the heart of Saint John's uptown core, the café features a variety of dining options such as a *prix fixe* menu on Saturday evening and half-price appetizers on Thursday evening (check the website for up-to-date information).

Chef Marcus Webster has created a menu to appeal to all tastes. Signature dishes of roasted rack of lamb or seafood fettuccini are complemented by creative soups and salads, plus a selection of starter or lighter-fare dishes, all made using fresh local ingredients.

Open daily for lunch and dinner
Restaurateurs: David Driscoll and Jeff Lee
43 Princess Street
Saint John, NB
Tel: (506) 693-2005
www.sebastiancafe.com

ST. MARTINS COUNTRY INN

Built in 1857, when St. Martins was a prosperous Bay of Fundy shipbuilding and trading centre, this replica of a Queen Anne villa was home to the William Vaughan family. Today this tranquil fishing port, with its covered bridges and gingerbread clapboard homes, is the gateway to the Fundy Trail Parkway. Locally referred to as "the Castle," St. Martins Country Inn provides guests with an elegant ambience. On-site Forget Me Not Gifts and Collectibles features New Brunswick pottery and crafts.

The dining room, furnished with splendid antiques, offers fine cuisine to guests and the general public.

Open April through October
Innkeepers: Albert and Myrna LeClair
St. Martins, NB
Tel: (506) 833-4534, 1-800-565-5257
www.stmartinscountryinn.com

SUWANNA RESTAURANT AND INN

The Suwanna Restaurant and Inn is located in a restored Victorian home overlooking the famous Reversing Falls and downtown Saint John. Originally built by lumberman Andrew Cushing in the mid-1800s, the building is an impressive structure, recently updated with modern amenities. The inn offers accommodation in six spacious rooms decorated in Victorian style.

At the restaurant, appetizers, soups and entrées reflect co-owner and Chef Jaruwan Gehrig's extensive experience in the art of Thai cuisine. Her husband Franz's European heritage is reflected in a mouth-watering selection of German-style desserts.

Inn open year round. Restaurant open daily for dinner (closed Monday)
Innkeepers/Restaurateurs: Jaruwan and Franz Gehrig
325 Lancaster Avenue
Saint John, NB
Tel: (506) 637-9015
www.suwanna.ca

renovations of late and currently offers luxurious accommodation in nine suites.

Under the direction of chef/sommelier Chris MacAdam the kitchen uses fresh land and sea ingredients to create offerings with an international flavour. A selection of fine wines is available to complement your dinner choice.

Open daily, year round for dinner
Innkeeper: Pierre Landry
293 Main Street
Shediac, NB
Tel: (506) 532-4233
www.maisontaithouse.com

THE WINDJAMMER RESTAURANT **15** AT DELTA BEAUSÉJOUR

Whether you select your dinner from the ever-changing menu or opt for *table d'hôte* service, you will enjoy fine dining at Moncton's Windjammer Restaurant located in the Delta Beauséjour, a full-service hotel.

The menu reflects attention to detail and features regional cuisine such as fresh Atlantic seafood, seasonal specialties, healthy heart options and vegetarian choices, all presented with flair. Desserts include pastries, crêpes, flambés, fresh fruits and cheeses. Wine suggestions for each course are offered, with some available by the glass.

Open Monday to Saturday for dinner
Delta Beauséjour Hotel
750 Main Street
Moncton, NB
Restaurant reservations: (506) 877-7137
www.deltabeausejour.com

THE TAIT HOUSE **11**

This impressive inn was built in 1911 as the residence of the Tait family, Shediac general merchants and international exporters of potatoes to South America and the Caribbean. In operation since 1980 as a country inn, the building has been treated to extensive

10 NOVA SCOTIA

In Nova Scotia, with its miles of coastline, one is always less than an hour's drive from the sea. What better place to enjoy cultural and geographical contrasts, from lazy days on the beach to hiking, sailing and golf, to perhaps dining in upscale urban eateries or small country inns. Take time to walk through the past at our many museums, tour a winery, schedule a whale-watching cruise or simply enjoy the cultural offerings of our towns and cities.

ACTON'S GRILL & CAFÉ 69

Acton's, a dining mecca in Wolfville since 1991, continues to provide locals and the many visitors to the Annapolis Valley with an exceptional dining experience.

Smartly decorated with antique ceramics and artwork prints of the internationally acclaimed local artist Alex Colville, you may choose to sit near the blazing fire in winter or on the terrace in summer. This upscale eatery offers a menu that changes with the seasons and reflects the abundance of local produce and Bay of Fundy seafood.

Open daily for lunch and dinner
Restaurateur/Chef: Drew Rudderham
268 Main Street
Wolfville, NS
Tel: (902) 542-7525
www.actons.ca

AMHERST SHORE COUNTRY INN

Located on the scenic shores of the Northumberland Strait in northeastern Nova Scotia, this small inn offers accommodation in its guest rooms and beachside cottages.

A four-course gourmet dinner is available to guests and the general public at a 7:30 pm sitting, by advance reservation. Everything is prepared on the premises and the chef makes excellent use of the inn's extensive gardens. The menu changes daily with a choice of a meat or seafood entrée and a rich or light dessert.

Open daily, May through October, off-season by request
Innkeepers: Robert and Mary Laceby
Lorneville, NS
Tel: (902) 661-4800, 1-800-661-2724
www.ascinn.ns.ca

BETWEEN THE BUSHES

This aptly named restaurant is indeed located amid the high-bush blueberry bushes of a working berry farm in rural Annapolis Valley. Diners may choose seating in the bright, airy dining room with its open kitchen or on the wrap-around deck with its superb pastoral views.

The culinary staff takes full advantage of the exceptional fresh produce, meats and seafood of the area, offering patrons a varied and well-executed menu. During strawberry and blueberry season make sure you save room for dessert. The strawberry shortcake with white chocolate whipped cream is sinful!

Open April 1 to mid-December. Monday and Tuesday, 11:30 am to 3:00 pm; Wednesday to Sunday, 11:30 am to 3:00 pm and 5:00 pm to 9:00 pm
Restaurateurs: The Kidston family
1225 Middle Dyke Road
Sheffield Mills, NS
Tel: (902) 582-3648
www.novaagri.com

BISH WORLD CUISINE ③⑦

Maurizio and Stephanie Bertossi's upscale restaurant can be found in the Bishop's Landing development on the Halifax Waterfront. The restaurant exudes a crisp, smart ambience with its pale woods, black accessories and broad glass windows that overlook the sparkling harbour. Bish specializes in "world cuisine," offering diners an innovative selection of meat, seafood and

vegetarian dishes expertly prepared and artfully presented in a relaxed yet elegant atmosphere.

If you enjoy dining at Bish, you will also enjoy the Bertossi's two companion restaurants, both named Il Mercato Ristorante, offering authentic Italian cuisine in a casual café setting.

Open year round, Monday to Saturday, 5:30 pm to 10:00 pm
Restaurateurs: Maurizio and Stephanie Bertossi
1475 Lower Water Street, Halifax, NS
Tel: (902) 425-7993
Il Mercato Ristorante, 5650 Spring Garden Road, Halifax and Sunnyside Mall, 1595 Bedford Highway, Bedford, NS
www.halifaxrestaurants.ca

THE BLOMIDON INN 70

Built in 1882 by Captain Rufus Burgess, this imposing inn features exotic woods, plaster cornices, dados and marble fireplaces fashioned by Italian craftsmen. The inn has 26 beautifully appointed guest rooms. Guests are invited to stroll through extensive gardens, sit on the patio or visit the on-site gift shop. Popular day trips from the inn include Grand Pré National

Historic Park, which commemorates the 1755 Expulsion of the Acadians, a hike to the breathtaking cliffs of Cape Split or a meander along the tree-lined streets of Wolfville.

The chefs at the Blomidon Inn pride themselves on preparing local cuisine, and the dining rooms feature an extensive wine list.

Open year round. Breakfast and afternoon tea for guests, lunch and dinner for guests and the general public
Innkeepers: James and Donna Laceby
127 Main Street
Wolfville, NS
Tel: (902) 542-2291, 1-800-565-2291
www.blomidoninn.ns.ca

CAFÉ CHRISTOPHE 27

Visitors looking for traditionally served, Acadian cuisine will find it at Café Christophe on Nova Scotia's French Shore. Walking through the back porch into the kitchen is like stepping back in time to a working-class Acadian home. The friendly staff may seat you in the original kitchen, the parlour or the dining room, where fortunate weekend guests may be entertained by a local musician and storyteller.

Restaurateur and chef Paul Comeau works diligently to create authentic Acadian dishes such as chicken fricot, fishcakes, rappie pie and fresh seafood. The restaurant is not licensed, but patrons are invited to bring their own wine. The owner also operates a charming bed and breakfast establishment nearby. Accommodation reservations may be made through the restaurant.

Open seasonally, Tuesday to Sunday, for breakfast, lunch and dinner

Restaurateur/chef: Paul Comeau
2655 Highway #1
Grosses Coques, NS
Tel: (902) 837-5817

CASTLE ROCK COUNTRY INN and AVALON THE RESTAURANT

Castle Rock Country Inn, perched high on a bluff overlooking the sparkling water of Ingonish Bay, has a panoramic view of Middle Head Peninsula. The inn is an ideal base for day trips to the Cape Breton Highlands National Park, the acclaimed Highland Links Golf Course and the Cabot Trail.

The inn features 17 gracious rooms and offers guests breakfast and special accommodation packages. Avalon the Restaurant is open to guests and the general public for lunch and dinner and features a variety of seasonal dishes including local seafood, poultry and lamb.

Open year round for breakfast, lunch and dinner
Innkeeper: Ian MacLennan
39339 Cabot Trail
Ingonish Ferry, NS
Tel: (902) 285-2700, 1-888-884-7625
www.ingonish.com/castlerock

with original works of art, oriental rugs and antique furniture.

Complimentary continental breakfast is included with lodging.

Gourmet dining, featuring selections made with organically grown ingredients, is offered to both guests and the general public by advance reservation. For those seeking a complete getaway, there are three one-bedroom housekeeping cottages located on the property.

Inn open May through October, off-season by request. Dining room open for dinner 7:00 pm to 9:00 pm
Innkeeper: Earlene Busch
48678 Cabot Trail
North River, St. Anns Bay, NS
Tel: (902) 929-2263, 1-866-277-0577
www.chanterelleinn.com

CHANTERELLE COUNTRY INN 61

A visit to Chanterelle Country Inn, with its tranquil atmosphere, is soothing to the soul. Sit back and enjoy a warm fire warding off the chills of early spring and late fall, or enjoy the gentle, cooling breezes as you relax on the screened veranda in summer. The inn has nine fully appointed and elegant guestrooms decorated

CHARLOTTE LANE CAFÉ AND CRAFTS

It is hard to believe that the sleepy little coastal town of Shelburne was the fourth-largest town in North America in the 1700s. Still, much of the charm and ambience of that bygone age remains evident in its proud old buildings and friendly inhabitants.

Swiss native Roland Glauser and his wife Kathleen operate the Charlotte Lane Café, a bright and cheerful restaurant located on a side street in town. Roland is an innovative chef who likes to use the best local produce, meats and seafood.

Open May through December, Tuesday to
Saturday, for lunch and dinner
Restaurateurs: Roland and Kathleen Glauser
13 Charlotte Lane
Shelburne, NS
Tel: (902) 875-3314
www.charlottelane.ca

CHIVES CANADIAN BISTRO 38

Tucked away in an old bank building in the heart
of downtown Halifax, Chives Canadian Bistro
offers a menu of "intense" comfort food, served
with flair.

While diners relax in the restaurant's casual
atmosphere they are treated to a creative menu
inspired by local ingredients as they come into
season. In the words of Chef Flinn, "Quality
ingredients are essential for quality menus."
Fresh seafood and meats, vegetables and fruits
from local farms are
found in dishes such
as the "hot pot," a
daily soup featuring
in-season produce
and the everchanging
seafood selection. All
entrées are served
with Chives'
signature buttermilk
biscuits. Chives also
offers special event
catering service.

Open daily, year
round, for dinner

Restaurateur/chef: Craig Flinn
1537 Barrington Street
Halifax, NS
Tel: (902) 420-9626
www.chives.ca

COCOA PESTO BISTRO AT THE 68 WOODSHIRE INN

A mere 40-minute drive from Halifax, Windsor
is fast becoming an easy commute for those who
prefer a more pastoral lifestyle. But there is
plenty to see and do in this historical Nova
Scotia town, as owners Scott Geddes and
Marilyn MacKay have found since relocating to
the area and opening their Cocoa Pesto Bistro
and Woodshire Inn. Windsor is home to a
variety of seasonal festivals, the Hockey Heritage
Centre, Kings-Edgehill School and Ski Martock.

The inn features two luxury suites. The
restaurant offers a varied menu, optimizing fresh
local produce, meats and seafood prepared in a
variety of cooking methods, including apple-
wood smoked entrées like signature dish Dry
Rub Pork Ribs.

Open year round. Dinner daily, 5:00 pm to 9:00
pm; lunch Monday through Friday, 11:30 am to
2:00 pm; brunch Saturday and Sunday, 10:00 am
to 2:00 pm
Innkeepers/Restaurateurs: Scott Geddes and
Marilyn MacKay
494 King Street
Windsor, NS
Tel: (902) 472-3300
www.cocoapesto.com

DA MAURIZIO DINING ROOM

Da Maurizio Dining Room occupies the lower level of a building that once housed Alexander Keith's brewery, known affectionately by locals as "the brewery."

Amid a setting of crisp linens, fine china and profuse greenery, da Maurizio's offers fine evening dining. The menu is varied and extensive, featuring flavourful northern Italian cuisine. Expect a wide range of appealing appetizers, salads, entrées and delectable desserts at this restaurant.

Open year round, Monday to Saturday, for dinner
Restaurateurs: Tanya and Andrew King
1496 Lower Water Street
Halifax, NS
Tel: (902) 423-0859
www.halifaxrestaurants.ca

DESBARRES MANOR COUNTRY INN

Situated in the quiet town of Guysborough, DesBarres Manor was built in the early 1830s by W. F. DesBarres, lawyer, judge and member of the Nova Scotia legislature. The manor was home to the DesBarres family until 1991. Today it has been meticulously restored to its past grandeur.

The inn features 10 luxurious rooms, beautifully decorated with period antiques. An extensive deck offers guests a panoramic view of the quiet countryside. The dining room, which serves in-house guests and the general public, offers a unique dining experience.

Open May through October
Innkeeper: Gwen Williams
90 Church Street
Guysborough, NS
Tel: (902) 533-2099, 1-877-818-7891
www.desbarresmanor.com

DIGBY PINES GOLF RESORT AND SPA

Originally part of Canadian Pacific Railway's chain of luxury destination resorts, the Pines is an elegant hotel set on a pine-covered hill overlooking the beautiful Annapolis Basin, a short distance from the Saint John-Digby ferry terminal. The Norman-style main hotel contains 84 tastefully decorated rooms and suites, while 30 cottages with living rooms and stone fireplaces are located nearby. The resort features a fitness centre, a heated outdoor pool, tennis courts, a platinum-rated golf course, lawn games, walking trails and a gift shop.

Breakfast, lunch and dinner are served in the hotel's Annapolis dining room or on the veranda. Award-winning executive chef and sommelier Claude AuCoin offers innovative French cuisine, including local delicacies from land and sea.

Resort open late May to mid-October.
Restaurant open for breakfast, lunch and dinner.
Manager: René LeBlanc
103 Shore Road
Digby, NS
Tel: (902) 245-2511, 1-800-667-4637
www.signatureresorts.com

DUNCREIGAN COUNTRY INN OF MABOU

Mabou may well have been a Scottish Highlander's idea of heaven in the New World. This little village on Cape Breton's Ceilidh Trail abounds with natural beauty and world-class hiking trails. It is also steeped in Gaelic culture and tradition. Situated among trees on the edge of Mabou's harbour, the Duncreigan Country Inn features eight bright and airy guest rooms graced with bowed windows that overlook either the saltwater estuary or the inn's gardens.

Buffet breakfast is served to guests only, although in the evening the dining room is open to guests and the public. In addition, The Mull Café & Deli, located in the village, offers lighter fare and full-service family-style dining. Using only the finest fresh products available, the owners have successfully married newer health-conscious trends with traditional Cape Breton fare.

Inn open year round. Dining room open mid-June to mid-October for dinner. The Mull Café & Deli open year round
Innkeepers: Charles and Eleanor Mullendore
Route 19 at Mabou Harbour, NS
Tel: (902) 945-2207, 1-800-840-2207
www.duncreigan.ca

EPICURIOUS MORSELS

Located in the trendy Hydrostone neighbourhood of Halifax's north end, this small and intimate bistro features French Mediterranean cuisine, specializing in seafood and unique salads. The restaurant offers the options of eating in or takeout.

The menu features a variety of soups, luncheon and dinner entrées and desserts. Look for the salmon, smoked or gravlax style, which is prepared in-house by the chef.

Open for lunch, Tuesday to Friday, 11:30 am to 3:00 pm; dinner, Tuesday to Saturday, 5:00 pm to 8:00 pm; brunch, Saturday and Sunday, 10:30 am to 2:30 pm
Restaurateurs: Jim Hanusiak and Linda Baldwin
5529 Young Street
Halifax, NS
Tel: (902) 455-0955
www.epicuriousmorsels.com

EVANGELINE CAFÉ

This little gem has long been a favourite for lunch or early supper with area locals. Informal seating is

available in the café or on an adjoining screened deck. Visitors to nearby Grand Pré National Historic Site will enjoy the homemade soups, salads, traditional sandwiches and pies. Drinks include yummy milkshakes and ice cream sodas.

The café is part of the Evangeline Inn and Motel complex, which offers five inn rooms with complimentary breakfast and 18 motel units.

Open daily, May through October,
8:00 am to 7:00 pm
Innkeeper: Sheila Carey
11668 Highway #1
Grand Pré, NS
Tel: (902) 542-2703, 1-888-542-2703
www.evangeline.ns.ca

FID 41

Dennis Johnston continues to create memorable meals for Halifax gourmands. His perfectly styled and executed traditional dishes, with global fusion accents, make a memorable dining experience. The menu changes frequently as dishes are created around the availability of fresh, prime ingredients. Patrons will always find unique appetizers, exquisitely prepared seafood and meat entrées and splendid desserts. Diners will long remember their meal in this bright, chic restaurant.

Open year round for lunch, Wednesday to Friday and dinner, Tuesday to Sunday
Restaurateurs: Chef Dennis Johnston, Maître d' Monica Bauche
1569 Dresden Row
Halifax, NS
Tel: (902) 422-9162
www.fidcuisine.ca

FIVE FISHERMEN 50

Five Fishermen has been a fixture of Halifax's dining scene for more than three decades. With its setting of brass, timber and stained glass, this warm, nautically decorated restaurant is located in the downtown core, a short walk from local hotels and entertainment venues. The award-winning menu emphasizes fresh Nova Scotia

seafood, produce and wines. A highlight of Five Fishermen is a visit to the mussel and salad bar.

For those seeking a more casual dining experience, visit Five Fishermen's companion on-site restaurant, Little Fish Restaurant and Oyster Bar.

Open Monday to Wednesday, 11:30 to midnight; Thursday to Saturday, 11:30 to 2:00 am; Sunday 4:00 pm to midnight
Manager: Gary MacDonald
1740 Argyle Street, Halifax
Tel: (902) 422-4421
www.fivefishermen.com
Little Fish Restaurant and Oyster Bar,
(902) 425-4025
www.littlefishrestaurant.ca

FLEUR DE SEL RESTAURANT

Visually stunning, this little gem of a restaurant is situated in the UNESCO designated heritage town of Lunenburg. The town, with its nautical heritage and quaint architecture, is a treasure. In this chic, upscale restaurant, owner/chef Martin Ruiz Salvador serves traditional French cuisine, expertly developed around a seasonal menu using local ingredients from both land and sea. The restaurant seats 30, and *al fresco* dining is offered seasonally on an outdoor patio.

A companion establishment, Salt Shaker Deli is located a short walk away at 124 Montague Street. At the deli you will find lighter fare, served with the same attention to detail, available to eat in or take out.

Open mid-April to December 31. Dinner: high season, daily, 5:00 pm to 10:00 pm; low season, Thursday to Sunday, 5:00 pm to 10:00 pm.
Brunch: Saturday and Sunday,
10:00 am to 2:00 pm
Restaurateurs: Martin Ruiz Salvador and Sylvie MacDonald
53 Montague Street

Lunenburg, NS
Tel: (902) 640-2121
www.fleurdesel.net

GABRIEAU'S BISTRO

Amid the hustle and bustle of a typical university town, Gabrieau's Bistro is a haven offering upscale lunch and dinner menus.

The two dining rooms, decorated in restful shades of pale yellow and accented with impressionist prints, are airy and bright. The varied selection of dishes reflects the chef's interest in fresh seafood, vegetables and meat. The menu offers innovative appetizers and the entree list includes several light pasta dishes, plus a wide array of traditional fare. Exceptional desserts complete the experience.

Open year round, Monday to Saturday,
for lunch and dinner
Restaurateur/Chef: Mark Francis Gabrieau
350 Main Street
Antigonish, NS
Tel: (902) 863-1925
www.gabrieaus.com

THE GARRISON HOUSE INN

Garrison House Inn is just one of many restored historic properties you will find as you stroll through the tranquil streets of Annapolis Royal. The French founded the town, Canada's oldest permanent settlement, in 1605. Annapolis Royal and its environs offer visitors live theatre, museums, golf and the Annapolis Royal Historic Gardens, one of Canada's finest theme gardens.

The inn was originally built in 1854 as the Temperance Hotel and features seven guestrooms. Well known for fine food, the inn offers nightly dining in three intimate dining rooms with *al fresco* service on the screened veranda in summer.

Open daily, May to October for dinner
(off season by appointment)
Innkeeper: Patrick Redgrave
350 St. George Street
Annapolis Royal, NS
Tel: (902) 532-5750
www.come.to/garrison

GIO 49

Everything about Gio can be summed up by the letter 'S.' From the restaurant's short, snappy name to the suave, stylish interior with its muted tones, accent art and collection of local art glass. The service is impeccable and the food superlative, both in taste and presentation.

Under the direction of Chef Ray Bear, you will be treated to uniquely crafted dishes with a global slant: delicious seafood soups and entrées, flavourful meat mains, appetizers and salads followed by sumptuous desserts, all complemented with a fine selection of wines and spirits.

Open Monday to Friday for lunch and dinner, Saturday for dinner only
Restaurateur: The Prince George Hotel; Chef: Ray Bear
1725 Market Street
Halifax, NS
Tel: (902) 425-1987
www.giohalifax.com

GOWRIE HOUSE COUNTRY INN 56

Gowrie House is a convenient starting point for touring Cape Breton and is only 15 minutes away from the Newfoundland ferry terminal. The Alexander Graham Bell Museum and Cabot Trail are less than an hour's drive away.

The inn offers 10 ensuite rooms and a caretaker's cottage that overlooks beautiful flower gardens. Decorated with fine antiques and original art, the house exudes a feeling of comfortable elegance. A full breakfast is included with lodging.

Gowrie House is known for its fine dining and uses the fresh produce from the fields, waters and gardens of Nova Scotia. Dinner is served to guests and the general public at a 7:30 pm sitting.

Inn open April to December. Dining room open for dinner daily (advance reservation only)
Innkeeper: Ken Tutty
840 Shore Road
Sydney Mines, NS
Tel: (902) 544-1050, 1-800-372-1115
www.gowriehouse.com

HAUS TREUBURG COUNTRY INN AND COTTAGES ⑥⑷

Georg and Elvie Kargoll fell in love with Cape Breton during a vacation in the early 1980s. Their plans to buy a vacation cottage ended with the purchase of a 1914 home and property on the shores of Port Hood — now Haus Treuburg Country Inn and Cottages. The inn offers three comfortable rooms and three adjacent one-bedroom cottages overlooking the water and Port Hood Island.

Breakfast is served to inn guests only, and a four-course *prix fixe* dinner is offered to guests and the general public. Chef and owner Georg prepares continental cuisine with German touches. Two softly lit dining rooms invite guests to spend a full evening of relaxing and enjoying the fine cuisine. Nightly sittings begin at 7:30 pm and feature varied entrées along with Georg's superbly prepared appetizers, soups, salads and desserts. All dishes are prepared in the inn's kitchen with the choicest of local products.

Inn open year round. Dinner offered June to October
Innkeepers: Georg and Elvie Kargoll

175 Main Street
Port Hood, NS
Tel: (902) 787-2116
www.haustreuburg.com

INVERARY RESORT ⑥②

Inverary Resort, one of four establishments operated by the MacAulay family, is located on the shores of the Bras d'Or Lakes in the village of Baddeck. This one-stop vacation centre for guests of all ages and interests offers a variety of facilities including tennis, canoeing, indoor pool, fitness centre and spa and convention centre.

Baddeck is a major tourist destination for boaters, golf enthusiasts and highway travellers. Of note is the Alexander Graham Bell Museum, looking out across the bay to Beinn Breagh, Bell's summer home for the last 37 years of his life. His descendants still own and vacation on the site.

Guests and the general public may dine at the Lakeside Café (seasonal), Flora's dining-room and the popular Celtic-style pub, which also offers nightly entertainment.

Inverary Inn has three companion establishments — Ceilidh Country Lodge in Baddeck, Glenghorm Beach Resort in Ingonish and Dundee Resort and Golf Club in West Bay — each offering its own brand of Cape Breton hospitality and cuisine.

Open May through November
Innkeeper: Scott MacAulay
368 Shore Road
Baddeck, NS
Tel: (902) 295-3500, 1-800-565-5660
www.capebretonresorts.com

JANE'S ON THE COMMON ④⓪

Owner Jane Wright has successfully brought her upscale version of a traditional neighbourhood restaurant to the Halifax dining scene. Located on the "opposite" side of the Halifax Common, away from the eateries of Spring Garden Road and downtown Halifax, the restaurant's chic black and red decor is lovingly overseen by a large reproduction of Lucas Cranch the Elder's "Venus" and a big chalkboard offering the day's delectable specials. Another wall sports a unique

black-and-white photo gallery of the owner and other Janes. You may also be afforded this honour if your name is Jane.

The restaurant claims to serve homestyle comfort food, but be prepared to enjoy fare that exceeds the norm in choice of ingredients, style and flavour. You will not find dishes like Cornbread Crusted Haddock, Grilled Pork Loin with Szechuan Shrimp and Scallop Sauce or Tahitian Vanilla Panna Cotta with Fresh Banana or Coconut-cream Pie with Shortbread Crust in most home kitchens. The menu also includes a varied selection of soups, salads and appetizers.

Open year round for lunch and dinner, Tuesday to Friday; brunch and dinner, Saturday; brunch, Sunday.
Restaurateur: Jane Wright

2394 Robie Street
Halifax, NS
Tel: (902) 431-5683
www.janesonthecommon.com

KELTIC LODGE RESORT AND SPA 58

In the late 1800s, Henry Corson of Akron, Ohio, exclaimed, "My dear that is the place!" He was referring to a spectacular, surf-tossed finger of land jutting out into the ocean — what the locals called Middle Head. The Corsons purchased the land, built a large log home, planted orchards and established a thriving dairy farm.

Today, the homestead has been replaced by Keltic's large white lodge and cozy cottages. Former cow pastures have been transformed into a world-class links-style golf course designed by Stanley Thompson, but the spectacular view of the ocean and mountains remain just as Henry Corson discovered it.

Resort open late May through October.
Restaurants open daily for breakfast, lunch and dinner
Manager: Walther Lauffer, Executive chef: Dale Nichols
Ingonish Beach, NS
Tel: (902) 285-2880, 1-800-565-0444
www.signatureresorts.com

La Co-opérative Artisanale was created in 1963 by a group of local artisans skilled in a style of rug hooking that has attracted international attention. Located on the harbour overlooking picturesque Cheticamp Island, the co-operative houses a museum, a gift store and the Acadian Restaurant. Waitresses in traditional costumes serve Acadian-style cuisine such as seafood, chowders, chicken fricot and meat pies, plus a varied selection of homemade pies and desserts.

Open daily, May to mid-October,
9:00 am to 9:00 pm
15067 Cabot Trail
Cheticamp, NS
Tel: (902) 224-2170
www.co-opartisanale.com

LA PERLA 53

La Perla is a charming restaurant located in Dartmouth's oldest commercial building, only a minute's walk from the ferry terminal. Many tables provide a view of downtown Halifax and the harbour.

Noted for its northern Italian cuisine, the dining room features a variety of dishes not often found in the metro area. Careful preparation using only the freshest of Nova Scotia seafood, local and imported fruits and vegetables, plus a selection of items from Italy and subtle European spices, ensures a delightful meal. Expect to find a variety of antipasti and soups, along with pasta, seafood, poultry and

meat entrées. Desserts at La Perla range from decadent cheesecake to gelato.

Open daily for dinner, Monday to Friday for lunch
Restaurateur: Pearl MacDougall
73 Alderney Drive
Dartmouth, NS
Tel: (902) 469-3241
www.laperla.ca

LA CO-OPÉRATIVE ARTISANALE- 59
ACADIAN RESTAURANT

Cheticamp is a proud and prosperous fishing village where the distinct blue, white and red striped Acadian flag flies above most establishments and French is the language of choice.

LISCOMBE LODGE RESORT AND CONFERENCE CENTRE 54

Liscombe Lodge lies hidden among the trees at the edge of a swiftly flowing river on Nova Scotia's Eastern Shore. Accommodation includes secluded chalets, European-style cottages and rooms in the Riverside Lodge, all with private balconies.

With boat, sea kayak and canoe rentals, tennis courts, an indoor pool, a playground and hiking trails, the resort offers a complete vacation experience. Staff will arrange for guided angling expeditions.

An informal veranda-style dining room with splendid views over the river is open to guests and the public for breakfast, lunch and dinner. The chefs at Liscombe Lodge prepare local dishes such as planked salmon, seafood chowders and desserts that utilize seasonal fruits and berries.

Open mid-May to mid-October for breakfast, lunch and dinner
Manager: Angela Steeves
Liscomb Mills, NS
Tel: (902) 779-2307, 1-800-665-6343
www.signatureresorts.com

MACKINNON-CANN HOUSE HISTORIC INN 28

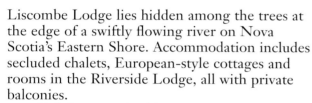

Yarmouth, with its seasonal ferry service to New England, is the gateway to Nova Scotia for many visitors. Whether you are arriving here by boat or car, a visit to the MacKinnon-Cann Inn will set the tone for a wonderful holiday. Lovingly

restored, the inn offers six ensuite rooms and several parlours decorated with 1880s Victoriana.

A continental breakfast is included for guests. The intimate, licensed dining rooms, serving lighter fare, are open to guests and the general public by reservation. The menu is ideal for those seeking a quiet respite following a busy day.

Inn open June to September. Dining rooms open for dinner, 5:30 pm to 10:00 pm, by reservation
Innkeepers: Neil Hisgen and Michael Tavares
27 Willow Street
Yarmouth, NS
Tel: (902) 742-9900
www.mackinnoncanninn.com

MILANO'S RISTORANTE 48

Milano's is an intimate gem of a restaurant situated unobtrusively in a neighbourhood of Halifax's central west end. Service is offered in two small dining rooms and — during pleasant weather — on the veranda.

The menu reflects Chef Peter Woodworth's attention to freshness and quality ingredients and changes with the season. Perhaps that is why Milano's has a following of regular patrons. Look for innovative soups, salads, pasta and main dishes, plus delectable desserts.

Open daily from 5:00 pm
Restaurateurs : Ron Lovett and Tom Hickey
6430 Chebucto Road
Halifax, NS
Tel: (902) 431-6500
www.milanosristorante.ca

NICKI'S INN CHESTER 35

Locals and returning visitors to Chester will be pleased to see that Nicki Butler, of the former Captain's House, is once again serving the public at Nicki's Inn in the heart of Chester Village. The inn offers accommodation with three bright and airy, elegantly appointed guestrooms. Dinner is served Wednesday to Saturday and a special, early dinner carvery operates on Sundays. Reservations are highly recommended.

Diners can expect superb innovative cuisine prepared with the finest fresh ingredients. Atlantic seafood is prominently featured in dishes such as Bouillabaisse and Halibut with Squash and Mushroom Risotto. Expect the menu to change frequently as the chef optimizes seasonal ingredients.

Inn open April through December. Dining room open Wednesday to Saturday, 5:00 pm to 9:00 pm; Sunday carvery 4:00 pm to 8:00 pm
Innkeeper: Judith Butler
26 Pleasant Street
Chester, NS
Tel: (902) 275-4342
www.aco.ca/nickis.html

THE NORMAWAY INN 60

Salmon anglers and travellers alike have been frequenting the Normaway Inn since 1928. Located in the beautiful Margaree Valley of the Cape Breton Highlands, this 100-hectare resort guarantees visitors instant immersion in the traditions and hospitality of the region.

The Normaway also offers weekly live entertainment by local Celtic musicians, many of whom have gained international recognition. Tennis courts, a recreation barn, lawn games and walking trails are also available.

The inn offers nine bedrooms with a common living room and library as well as 17 one- and two-bedroom cabins. The dining room, open to guests and the general public, serves gourmet country cuisine, specializing in local meats, seafood and produce from the inn's garden.

Open mid-June to mid-October
Innkeeper: David MacDonald
691 Egypt Road
Margaree Valley, NS
Tel: (902) 248-2987, 1-800-565-9463
www.normaway.com

OAK ISLAND RESORT AND SPA 34

Situated on the shores of beautiful Mahone Bay, Oak Island Resort is a full-service holiday destination offering accommodation in 97 hotel units, 10 suites and 13 two-bedroom chalets. Suitable for corporate meetings, family gatherings or intimate getaways, the resort offers an indoor pool, a spa, tennis courts and a marina.

The dining room at the inn presents traditional Nova Scotian fare such as fresh lobster, steamed mussels and seafood, as well as an array of poultry and meat entrées. A children's menu is available.

Resort open year round. Dining room open for
breakfast, lunch and dinner
Innkeeper: Dan Myers
Western Shore, NS
Tel: (902) 627-2600, 1-800-565-5075
www.oakislandresortandspa.com

OLD ORCHARD INN AND SPA 72

A visit to the Acadian Room Restaurant of the
Old Orchard Inn in Greenwich is a must for
travellers to the Annapolis Valley. An indoor
pool, spa services, sundeck, tennis and
playground are but a few of the inn's amenities.
This complex consists of 100 hotel rooms plus
29 cabins, making it an ideal stop for romantic
getaways, families or business conferences.
    Situated on a hill with a panoramic view of
Cape Blomidon and the ever changing tides of
the Minas Basin, the inn serves breakfast, lunch
and dinner to guests and the general public.
The menu, which changes with the seasons,
features healthy options using fresh valley
produce and seafood.

Open year round
Innkeepers: The Wallace family
153 Greenwich Road South (exit #11 from
Highway 101)
Greenwich, NS
Tel: (902) 542-5751, 1-800-561-8090
www.oldorchardinn.com

ONYX DINING ROOM AND COCKTAIL LOUNGE 52

Onyx offers big-city chic within intimate
surroundings. Located in Halifax's trendy retail
and entertainment area, this restaurant and bar
features a sleek and modern decor.

When dining at Onyx you can choose a
drink and a snack from the sharing platters or
order a two- or three-course dinner from the
prix fixe menu that changes weekly. Patrons will
enjoy a fusion of innovative Asian-influenced
French cuisine presented with flair.

Open Monday to Wednesday, 4:30 pm to 11:00
pm; Thursday to Saturday, 4:30 pm to 1:00 am
Restaurateur: RCR Hospitality Group
5680 Spring Garden Road
Halifax, NS
Tel: (902) 428-5680
www.onyxdining.com

OPA GREEK TAVERNA 46

University friends Costa Elles and Chris
Tzaneteas opened their Greek taverna in Halifax
in 2000. For those familiar with the bustle and
warmth of a Greek family restaurant, Opa,
which is located in a busy downtown corridor of
bars and eateries, is a culinary delight.
    Look for authentic fare such as dolmades,
spanakopita, moussaka, souvlaki and baklava.
The menu, which includes a children's section, is
extensive and sure to please all tastes.

Open for lunch and dinner Monday to Saturday
from 11:00 am; dinner only Sunday from 4 pm

Restaurateurs: Costa Elles and Chris Tzaneteas
1565 Argyle Street
Halifax, NS
Tel: (902) 492-7999
www.opataverna.com

THE PALLISER RESTAURANT, ㊻ MOTEL & GIFTS

The Palliser complex sits on land settled by British pioneers in 1760 — the first English-speaking people to arrive in the area. Today, the pastoral setting is an ideal spot for viewing the Bay of Fundy tidal bore. This natural phenomenon, created by the unique geography of the bay, occurs twice daily when a bore of water rushes upriver and crashes against the banks and rocks. Staff at the Palliser will gladly indicate the best times and sites for viewing.

This 40-unit motel offers modest accommodation, an extensive gift shop and a restaurant that reflects Nova Scotia hospitality at its very best. The Palliser has been serving homestyle meals in its charming dining room for several decades. Look for a menu featuring homemade soups, meat and seafood entrées and an array of tasty desserts.

Open May through October for breakfast, lunch and dinner.

Restaurateurs: Keltie and Allan Bruce
Tidal Bore Road (Exit 14, Highway 102)
Truro, NS
Tel: (902) 893-8951
www.palliserrestaurantmotelandgifts.ca

PIPER'S LANDING ㊻

Owners Matt and Brenda Vohs invite guests to relax and enjoy the ambience of their establishment on the East River near the historic town of Pictou. Tables near the windows overlook lawns that flow down to the water's edge. This is a beautiful scene that changes with the seasons.

The Vohs serve fine country-style cuisine that is never rushed out of the kitchen. Enjoy

freshly prepared salads with homemade dressings, freshly made soups and chowders and entrées ranging from roast turkey with all the trimmings to fresh Atlantic haddock prepared blackened, poached or pan-fried.

Open year round for dinner, 5:00 pm to 9:00 pm daily, except Thursdays
Restaurateurs: Matt and Brenda Vohs
Rte. 376
Lyon's Brook, NS
Tel: (902) 485-1200

QUARTERDECK BEACHSIDE ㉚ VILLAS AND GRILL

The sound of the surf, the smell of fresh salt air and the view of Summerville Beach are all included in a stay at the Quarterdeck, a resort offering a collection of one-bedroom suites, luxury

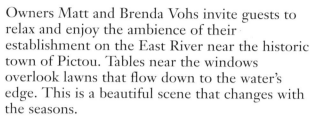

two-bedroom villas and a three-bedroom cottage.

The Quarterdeck Grill has become one of the most popular places to dine on the South Shore. The restaurant is known for its lobster and seafood dishes, such as planked salmon and the extravagant lobster tail stuffed with shrimp and scallops. Be prepared to find a varied menu of delectable soups, salads, entrées and desserts. The food is wonderful and the atmosphere bright and folksy.

Villas open year round. Dining room open daily for lunch and dinner, mid-May to mid-October
Owner: Doug Fowler
Summerville Beach, NS
Tel: (902) 683-2998, 1-800-565-1119
www.quarterdeck.ns.ca

RESTAURANT LE CAVEAU AT (73) DOMAINE DE GRAND PRÉ

Nestled in the rolling hills of Grand Pré and sheltered from the Bay of Fundy by Cape Blomidon, this winery offers tours, tastings and an enjoyable dining experience in a beautiful setting.

Whether seated among the columns of the pergola overlooking the vineyard or in the intimate dining room, guests are sure to enjoy the seasonal dishes, meticulously prepared with a Swiss flair.

Open May through December for lunch and dinner.
Restaurant Manager: Beatrice Jurt
Grand Pré, NS
Tel: (902) 542-7177
www.grandprewines.ns.ca

RHUBARB GRILL AND CAFÉ (36)

Rhubarb overlooks protected coastal woodland marked by giant granite rocks and wild flowers, and is part of the Oceanstone Inn and Cottages by the Sea complex. The inn, located a stone's throw from the sea, offers 10 guest rooms and suites as well as housekeeping cottages, all with fireplaces and private decks.

Rhubarb Grill features fine dining under the direction of Chef Paul MacInnis. Menu highlights are fresh coastal seafood and very special desserts made on the premises. This restaurant encourages satisfied diners to linger by the fireside and truly savour their meal.

Inn open year round. Restaurant open daily June to mid-September for dinner.
Innkeepers: Ron and Carole MacInnis
Restaurateur/Chef: Paul MacInnis
8650 Peggy's Cove Road
Indian Harbour, NS
Tel: (902) 823-2160, 1-866-823-2160
www.rhubarbgrill.com

SÆGE BISTRO

Located in the residential area of Spring Garden Road near the hospitals, Dalhousie University and the Public Gardens, Saege Bistro is the latest restaurant in the Scanway Catering Company holdings. Operated by Geir Simensen, son of well known Halifax restaurateur Unni Simensen this restaurant is an oasis of tranquility with its subtle green decor and urban garden atmosphere.

The menu features a varied selection of unique bistro-style fare including sandwiches, salads, light luncheon and dinner fare. Featured ingredients are drawn from all corners of the world, creating a menu that is sure to offer whatever your taste desires. The desserts are delectable.

Companion restaurants are Sweet Basil Bistro, located at 1866 Upper Water Street and Cheapside Café located in the Art Gallery of Nova Scotia at 1723 Hollis Street.

Open 11:00 am to 10:00 pm, Tuesday to Friday, 8:00 am to 10:00 pm Saturday and Sunday, closed Monday
Chef/Restaurateur: Geir Simensen

5883 Spring Garden Road
Halifax, NS
Tel: (902) 429-1882
www.saege.ca

SEASIDE SHANTY RESTAURANT 33

This delightful little restaurant, noted for its fresh seafood, is perched at the water's edge in Chester

Basin and is popular with both the locals and the yachting crowd. Patrons are invited to dock their watercraft at the adjacent municipal wharf.

Service at the Seaside Shanty is casual. Tables are available on the interior, covered patio or on the oceanside deck. The menu includes light fare of chowders and salads as well as heartier entrées such as assorted stir-fry dishes, steaks, chicken or knockwurst served with sauerkraut from nearby Tancook Island.

Open daily May through October for lunch and dinner
Restaurateurs: Rodney and Elizabeth Buell
5315 Highway #3
Chester Basin, NS
Tel: (902) 275-2246

SEVEN 42

Located on Grafton Street near major hotels and the Neptune Theatre, Seven is a newer entrant on Halifax's dining scene. A perfect blend of old and new, the restaurant sports a sleek modern interior within a classic brick structure.

The restaurant offers service on two levels plus a warm-weather patio. The upscale menu features an eclectic selection of North

1579 Grafton Street
Halifax, NS
Tel: (902) 444-4777
www.sevenwinebar.com

American, Thai and Eastern cuisine, and the extensive wine list boasts more than 60 selections served by the glass.

Open year round, Monday to Saturday, 11 am to midnight; Sunday, 4:00 pm to midnight. Lunch 11:00 am to 4:00 pm
Restaurateurs: Costa Elles and Chris Tzaneteas

STORIES AT THE HALLIBURTON

Stories is located at the Halliburton House Inn, a small elegant hotel on a quiet street in downtown Halifax. Built between 1809 and 1860, the inn comprises three registered heritage townhouses joined by a backyard flagstone patio. Each has been impeccably restored to its former elegance and decorated appropriately in period antiques.

The menu at Stories showcases fresh seafood and wild game in a variety of perfectly prepared appetizers, salads and entrées. The chef's luxurious desserts are tempting finales to any meal.

Inn open year round. Dining room open daily for dinner
Innkeeper: Robert Pretty
5184 Morris Street
Halifax, NS
Tel: (902) 420-0658
www.halliburton.ns.ca

TEMPEST WORLD CUISINE

In the heart of Wolfville, Tempest offers a unique interpretation of world cuisine under the artful guidance of owner and chef Michael Howell and his wife Mary Harwell. Advocates of the slow food movement, they offer a lunch menu of authentically prepared ethnic foods at affordable prices.

Dinner offerings showcase Chef Howell's

TRATTORIA DELLA NONNA 32
RISTORANTE E PIZZERIA

In keeping with the quaint architecture of Lunenburg, this restaurant encompasses three levels of a century-old building, transforming it into an oasis of warmth and style. The town is a destination point for travellers interested in the North Atlantic seafaring era, early New World architecture and rugged coastal beauty. Though steeped in history, Lunenburg is a thriving working community where the paths of tourists and locals frequently cross.

The extensive menu offers classic Italian fare including pasta, salads, thin-crust wood-fired pizza, principal entrées and sumptuous desserts. The service is attentive and you have to pinch yourself to realize you are not in Tuscany!

Open for lunch Tuesday to Friday from 11:30 am; dinner Tuesday to Saturday from 5:00 pm; brunch, Sunday from 10:30 am
Restaurateurs: Simone Mombourquette and Terry Vassallo
9 King Street
Lunenburg, NS
Tel: (902) 640-3112
www.nonnadining.ca

multicultural cooking talents with recipes that blend cuisines from around the globe. Diners can enjoy these relaxed repasts in the tranquil dining room, in a glassed-in porch or seasonally on the patio under towering elms and grape vines.

Open daily, year round for lunch and dinner.
Spanish tapas Friday and Saturday 9:00 to 11:00 pm
Restaurateur/Chef: Michael Howell
117 Front Street
Wolfville, NS
Tel: (902) 542-0588, 1-866-542-0588
www.tempest.ca

11 PRINCE EDWARD ISLAND

Whether you arrive by ferry, bridge or air, there is something magical about Prince Edward Island, the land Canadians lovingly call "The Garden of the Gulf." The houses are painted a white that is brighter than sunlight, and the green grass and red soil are of deeper hues than any found elsewhere in Canada. Our restaurant and inn selections were chosen to offer the total Island experience, from upscale inns offering gourmet fare to cozy cafés offering hospitality and comfort food — Island style. We strongly suggest you try one of the many lobster suppers served in church halls and community centres across the island, and plan a visit to the Lucy Maud Dining Room at the Culinary Institute of Canada in Charlottetown, where senior students prepare and serve meals under the watchful eye of their instructors.

CLADDAGH OYSTER HOUSE 78

Established in 1983 in the heart of Charlottetown, the Claddagh Oyster House offers a varied dinner menu including pasta, meats and the house specialties — succulent, fresh Island oysters and seafood. The restaurant is warm and intimate with attentive service.

Casual dining, with lighter pub fare such as pot pies, steamed mussels and chowders, is offered upstairs in the Olde Dublin Pub. The pub also features live Irish and Maritime music.

Open year round, Monday through Saturday,
5:00 pm to 10:00 pm
Restaurateurs: Liam Dolan and John Bill
Tel: (902) 892-9661
www.claddaghoysterhouse.com
The Olde Dublin Pub: open daily, year round for
lunch and dinner, except Sunday (dinner only)
Tel: (902) 892-6992
131 Sydney Street
Charlottetown, PE
www.oldedublinpub.com

DALVAY BY THE SEA

Built by Alexander MacDonald at the end of the
nineteenth century, Dalvay is one of the
Maritimes' most elegant country inns. Rich
wood panelling, a giant sandstone fireplace and
rooms filled with antiques await guests, while the
warm waters and sweeping dunes of Dalvay
Beach National Park are just a stone's throw
away. Additional accommodations are available
in eight 3-bedroom executive cottages newly
built on the inn's property. Tennis courts,
croquet greens, bike rentals and trails plus miles
of spectacular beaches are but a few of the
amenities at Dalvay.

Accommodations are modified American
plan, offering guests breakfast and dinner daily.
The elegant dining room, specializing in local
seafood, the freshest produce and the most
delectable desserts, is open to the general public
for breakfast, lunch and dinner.

Open June through mid-October
Innkeeper: David Thompson
Grand Tracadie, PE
Tel: (902) 672-2048, 1-888-366-2955
www.dalvaybythesea.com

DAYBOAT RESTAURANT

Located in the tranquil village of Oyster Bed
Bridge, this award-winning restaurant offers a
refined dining experience with cuisine that is

truly the essence of the Island. The menu, under
the expert hands of chef Sean Furlong, features
the freshest island ingredients from land and sea
— oysters, mussels, lobster, pork, beef and
poultry, all artistically prepared with an
accompanying sampling of island vegetables.
Diners may choose from a sampling menu,
entree menu or the chef's five-course table.
Reservations are strongly recommended.

Open: June through October, noon to 10:00 pm
Restaurateur: Robert Shapiro
5033 Rustico Road
Rte. 6 at Oyster Bed Bridge, PE
Tel: (902) 963-3833
www.dayboat.ca

THE DUNDEE ARMS INN

The Dundee Arms Inn is a full-service
establishment offering country-style charm in
the heart of historic Charlottetown. Built in
1903 as a private mansion, the structure is an
example of the Queen Anne Revival architectural
style. There are eight guest rooms and three

The café at the Dunes Gallery offers one of the Island's best dining experiences. The chefs grow their own herbs, vegetables and edible flora. In addition to local produce, diners enjoy meats and seafood expertly prepared and innovatively presented on the studio's handmade dishes.

The café is part of a multi-level glass and wood gallery and pottery studio. Visitors may purchase a wide selection of original art, jewellery, furniture and crafts, as well as the award winning stoneware, tableware and sculpture of owner Peter Jansons and his associate Joel Mills.

Open daily, mid-June through September for lunch and dinner
Brackley Beach Road
Brackley Beach, PE
Tel: (902) 672-1883
www.dunesgallery.com

suites in the inn, plus additional fully serviced accommodation in an adjacent motel.

Diners may choose from service in the Griffon Dining Room or the casual Hearth and Cricket Pub and its seasonal deck, open to guests and the general public.

Open daily, year round for breakfast, lunch and dinner
Innkeeper: Patricia Sands
200 Pownal Street
Charlottetown, PE
Tel: (902) 892-2496, 1-877-638-6333
www.dundeearms.com

THE DUNES CAFÉ AND **86** STUDIO GALLERY

FLEX MUSSELS **81**

What is Prince Edward Island most famous for? Anne of Green Gables? Well, yes, but we are talking about food, and the Island is famous for

succulent mussels and potatoes. Welcome to Charlottetown's newest restaurant, Flex Mussels, where chef Garner Quain offers not one but 23 versions of mussels on his menu. That means you will have to return 22 times to sample them all!

Situated on Charlottetown's waterfront, this 120-seat restaurant serves mussels, hand-cut and deep-fried PEI Russet Burbank potatoes, and for those not daring enough to try mussels, the menu features a unique lobster roll.

Open mid-May through September,
noon to late evening
Restaurateurs: Robert and Laura Shapiro,
Garner and Meg Quain
2 Lower Water Street
Charlottetown, PE
Tel: (902) 569-0200
www.flexmussels.com

THE GAHAN HOUSE 79

At the Gahan House microbrewery and eatery,
patrons may enjoy a pint of handcrafted beer or
ale with their lunch or dinner. Situated in the
original nineteenth-century brick residence of
general merchant John Gahan, the pub has a
modern eclectic atmosphere that blends well
with the imposing architecture. Diners may
choose seating in a variety of alcoves and small

rooms or on the patio. The pub's bistro-style
dishes often feature its microbrew ale or beer as
an ingredient.

Open daily, year-round for lunch and dinner
Owners: The Murphy Group
126 Sydney Street
Charlottetown, PE
Tel: (902) 626-2337
www.peimenu.com

THE HOME PLACE INN AND 83
RESTAURANT

Situated in the village of Kensington, a mere 25
km from the Cavendish entrance to PEI

National Park, this lovingly restored home was
once the residence of merchant Parmenus Orr.
If you appreciate the past you will enjoy reliving
the rich history of the Orr era, as many of the
original paintings, photographs and antiques
remain at the inn.

The licensed dining room and pub serve
home cooking at its best, to guests and the
public. Special allowances are made for those
with dietary concerns. You will enjoy baked rolls,
muffins and desserts that have been prepared on
the premises, plus the freshest of island produce,
seafood and meats.

Inn open year round, breakfast included. Dining
room open June 1 to Labour Day, noon to 9:00 pm
Innkeeper: Glenda Burt
21 Victoria Street East
Kensington, PE
Tel: (902) 836-5686, 1-866-522-9900
www.peisland.com/homeplace/

THE INN AT BAY FORTUNE 90

Situated on 18 hectares of land overlooking Bay
Fortune as it opens out to the Northumberland
Strait, the inn is 13 kilometres from the
Magdalen Islands' ferry in Souris and 72
kilometres from Charlottetown.

The lodge was built in 1910 as the summer
hideaway of playwright Elmer Harris, author of
the 1940s Broadway hit *Johnny Belinda*. It now
features 11 spacious suites, each with a view of
the sea and a romantic sitting area with fireplace.
A four-story tower includes a common room,
observatory and telescope. The owner's
companion establishment, Inn at Spry Point, just
off Rte. 310, features luxury accommodation, fine

Bay Fortune, PE
Tel: (902) 687-3745
www.innatbayfortune.com

THE OLDE GLASGOW MILL (84) RESTAURANT

History abounds in this century-old building. Erected in 1893 as the New Glasgow Hall Company, it has been a courthouse, community hall and schoolhouse — we would know everything about the area if only the walls could whisper!

Today, the restaurant provides fine dining featuring succulent island seafood, meats and produce. A children's menu is available. Situated in a pastoral setting the restaurant has two dining rooms and a second floor sunroom and deck, all overlooking the scenic River Clyde.

Open daily, June to September, 11:30 am to 9:30 pm
Restaurateurs: Rosemary and Harvey Larkin
Rte. 13 at New Glasgow, PE
Tel: (902) 964-3313
www.peisland.com/oldemill/

dining, ocean frontage and walking trails. There are three world-class golf courses in the vicinity.

Abundant gardens surround the property, providing the restaurant with vegetables and herbs. Breakfast is reserved for guests only, but the dining room is open to guests and the general public each evening.

Open daily, late May to mid-October for breakfast (Inn guests only) and dinner
Innkeeper: David Wilmer

THE PILOT HOUSE 80

Housed in one of Charlottetown's exceptional heritage buildings, this classy establishment offers two distinct dining experiences under the same roof.

Turn right at the entrance and you enter a softly lit dining room with seating in a variety of upholstered booth, banquette and table settings. Here diners may choose from a selection of expertly prepared first courses, seafood and meat entrées and delicious desserts.

A left turn at the entrance leads to an elegant, yet relaxed pub serving meals that match the refined decor in quality and presentation. Owner Doug Harvey is the son of legendary hockey great Doug Harvey, and NHL fans will be impressed with the tasteful collection of Montreal Canadiens memorabilia.

Open year round, Monday to Saturday, 11:30 am to midnight; food service 11:30 am to 10:00 pm
Owners: Doug and Judy Harvey
70 Grafton Street
Charlottetown, PE
Tel: (902) 894-4800
www.thepilothouse.ca

SHAW'S HOTEL 87

Four generations of the Shaw family have provided relaxing country lodging for Island visitors. The original farmhouse, a lodge and 17 cottages on the property are decorated in traditional Island style. Famed Brackley Beach, with its pink sand and windswept dunes, is a short walk from the hotel through a shaded lane.

Daily rates include meals, and the dining room is also open to the public by reservation. Fresh Atlantic lobster, salmon, scallops, prime rib and Prince Edward Island lamb are but a few of the offerings on the extensive menu.

Open June through September
Innkeepers: Robbie and Pam Shaw
Brackley Beach, PE
Tel: (902) 672-2022
www.shawshotel.ca

STANHOPE BEACH RESORT 88

Visitors will enjoy the vista of Covehead Bay from the verandas of this restored historic resort. Located 20 minutes from Charlottetown, the Stanhope Beach Resort is a short walk from the Stanhope entrance to the PEI National Park or Stanhope Golf and Country Club.

The resort features 86 guest rooms in a main lodge or cottages, and is an ideal family destination offering a pool, tennis, croquet and playground. In-house guests are served a continental breakfast included in the room rate. In the dining room guests and the general public are offered Island produce and seafood that has been harvested nearby.

Resort open mid-May to mid-October. Dining room open for dinner daily from 5:00 pm
Innkeepers: Mike Murphy and Paul Smith
3445 Bayshore Road
York, PE
Tel: (902) 672-2701
www.stanhopebeachresort.com

VICTORIA VILLAGE INN AND RESTAURANT 82

A small village on the Northumberland Strait, a mere half-hour from Borden, Charlottetown or Cavendish, Victoria-by-the-Sea is home to live theatre, galleries and antique and craft shops.

Next door to the Victoria Playhouse, the Village Inn offers accommodation in four spacious guest rooms. Breakfast is for in-house guests only, but the dining room serves classic French and Italian cuisine to guests and the general public for dinner. Dinner and theatre packages are available.

Open June 1 to September 30
Innkeeper: Stephen Hunter
22 Howard Street
Victoria-by-the-Sea, PE
Tel: (902) 658-2483
www.victoriavillageinn.com

WINDOWS ON THE WATER CAFÉ 91

Overlooking the Montague River, Windows on the Water offers friendly service and flavourful meals. Seating is available in a small dining room decorated with local antiques or *al fresco* on the wraparound deck.

The menu features casual fare, highlighting local seafood such as Island blue mussels, lobster, crab and haddock as well as fresh produce from Island farms. Though the servings are generous, try to save room for homemade dessert.

Open daily, May through September,
for lunch and dinner
Restaurateurs: Betty Higgins and Lillian Gurnham
Corner of Sackville and Main Streets
Montague, PE
Tel: (902) 838-2080

LOCATOR MAP

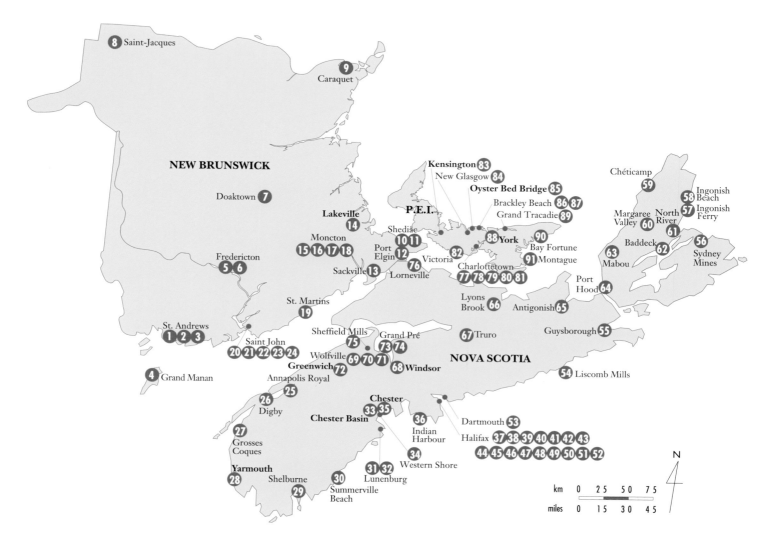

NEW BRUNSWICK

Caraquet
   9 Hotel Paulin
Doaktown
   7 The Ledges Inn
Fredericton
   5 The Blue Door Restaurant
    and Bar
   6 Caribbean Flava's Casual
    Fine Dining
Grand Manan
   4 Inn at Whale Cove Cottages
Lakeville

14 Le Flair Restaurant at
   Wild Rose Inn
Moncton
   15 The Windjammer Restaurant
    at Delta Beauséjour
   16 Bogart's Bar and Grill
   17 Pastilli Italian Cucina
   18 Little Louis' Oyster Bar
Port Elgin
   12 Little Shemogue Country Inn
Sackville
   13 Marshlands Inn
Saint-Jacques

8 Auberge les Jardins Inn
Saint John
   20 Billy's Seafood Company
   21 Suwanna Restaurant and Inn
   22 Inn on the Cove & Spa
   23 Opera Bistro
   24 Sebastian
St. Andrews
   1 The Fairmont Algonquin
   2 Inn on Frederick
   3 Rossmount Inn
St. Martins
   19 St. Martins Country Inn

INDEX